T0106209

SHORT ESSAYS ON YOUR ENEMY'S VICIOUS THOUGHTS

Sadistic Thinking from Mankind's Invisible Stalker

BOB JACKSON

WESTBOW
PRESS
A DIVISION OF THOMAS NELSON

WestBow Press books may be ordered through booksellers or by contacting:

WestBow Press
A Division of Thomas Nelson
1663 Liberty Drive
Bloomington, IN 47403
www.westbowpress.com
1-(866) 928-1240

Because of the dynamic nature of the Internet, any web addresses or links contained in this book may have changed since publication and may no longer be valid. The views expressed in this work are solely those of the author and do not necessarily reflect the views of the publisher, and the publisher hereby disclaims any responsibility for them.

Any people depicted in stock imagery provided by Thinkstock are models, and such images are being used for illustrative purposes only.

Certain stock imagery © Thinkstock.

ISBN: 978-1-4497-3497-8 (sc)
ISBN: 978-1-4497-3496-1 (e)

Library of Congress Control Number: 2011963158

Printed in the United States of America

WestBow Press rev. date: 1/19/2012

Contents

"Stay alert! Watch out for your great enemy, the devil, He prowls around like a roaring lion, looking for someone to devour", 1 Peter 5:8 (NLT 2nd Ed.).

Robert E Jackson © 2011

Preface and Acknowledgement

"God's Word is His thoughts written down on paper for our study and consideration. His Word is how He thinks about every situation and subject", (Meyers, 1995, p.167).

We also get a good indication of what the thoughts of our enemy are from God's Word and we are warned to be alert to his many deceptions and murderous intentions.

I would like to thank Father God for creating His amazing plan of redemption and salvation for His children.

I would like to thank the Lord Jesus Christ for His obedience to the Father by becoming the Lamb of God who took away the sins of the world.

I would like to thank the Holy Spirit who is presently with us, comforting, teaching, speaking, guiding and being the catalyst for our spiritual transformation.

I would like to thank my daughter Genne for volunteering to use her God given talent as an artist in producing the art work for the angel as shown on the back cover for these essays.

Finally, I want to thank my beloved wife Juliane for helping me write these essays. She is truly a woman who fears the Lord and is faithfully an excellent wife as described in Proverbs 31:10-31.

The Author

Robert E Jackson is a certified Lay
Teacher and Trainer of the Evangelism
Explosion III International Equipping
Ministry, a ministry created and founded by Dr. D. James Kennedy. The EE
ministry is intended for lay-witnessing. It features teaching, leadership, and
training believers in Christ to learn and to present the gospel effectively in
a non-offensive manner. In addition, Bob has studied personal evangelism
at the Moody Bible Institute Correspondence School and has been actively
engaged in spiritual warfare by following the biblical principal as written
in 2 Tim. 2:15.

These essays are Bob's first public writing under the influence and guidance
of the Holy Spirit. They are vivid essays with footnotes at the bottom of
each page. With each essay are comments, a pause for the reader to think,
to watch and pray concerning the words that address each essay. This
format is designed to teach by studying the scripture applications associated
with each paragraph and to remind the Christian believer in Christ to be
prepared and ready for spiritual warfare. The enemy is cunningly deceptive.
You must be clothed in the armor of God always, Eph. 6:10-18.

Bob and his wife Juliane reside in Delaware, USA and are actively and
faithfully involved in doing good works (Titus 3:14), (James 2:26),
(Proverbs 21:13). They support the expansion of the Kingdom of the
Lord Jesus Christ by utilizing the lessons learned from the "Parable of
the Talents" as recorded in (Matthew 25:14-30), and they are currently
serving as ambassadors of the Kingdom in accordance with (2 Corinthians
5:20).

Forward

What are the thoughts of the enemy of God concerning the entire human race?

The answer to this question is that his thoughts are to steal, kill, and destroy; He is the ultimate thief in human history. He will steal your possessions, your love ones, your parents, your family, and your friends. He will steal your health, steal your wealth, steal your reputation, steal your means of making a living and steal your joy of life. He is the unseen ruler of this world.[1]

How does the enemy kill? How does he slay, murder, slaughter, execute, destroy, exterminate, eradicate, and assassinate. How does he massacre and dispatch members of the human race? He and his demons accomplish this by continuously attacking Gods creation, especially humans by promoting every form of deceit and everything that God disapproves with the intent of destroying life especially the lives of those who refuse to love the truth.[2]

How does the enemy destroy? How does he defeat, crush, subdue, demolish, annihilate, overcome, overthrow and wipe out the unbelieving populations of adults and the innocent on planet earth. He does this through hate. The enemy hates God and he hates what God loves, he hates integrity, he hates creation, and he hates Zion, he especially hates those who love God, because God is love.[3]

---

1   Job 1:1-22 (NIV), Job 2:1-11 (NIV), John 10:10 (NIV), Eph.2:2 (NIV), 2 Cor. 4:4 (NIV)
2   Rev. 12:9 (NIV), Hosea 4:2 (BIBE), 2 Thess. 2:10 (GWT), John 14:6 (ESV)
3   Prov. 29:10 (BIBE), Psa. 69:4 (WEB), Psa. 129:5 (NIV), 1 John 4:20 (ESV), 1 John 4:8 (NIV), 1 John 3:17 (NIV), 1 John 4:16 (NIV)

The following are a series of short descriptive essays on the thoughts and plots of the enemy who wants to destroy Love and all of His Creation. Following each essay are comments, think about each essay, what are your thoughts. Let these essays remind you to take on the whole armor of God and be ready to stand against the evil one, by knowing, understanding, teaching, speaking and applying the WORD as you go about your everyday life.[4]

---

4   Eph. 6:11 (NIV), John 1:1 (NIV)

Introduction

The purpose and goal of these essays are to remind the Saints of what the scriptures have to say about their adversary the devil. He is described as prowling around, roaring and looking for someone to devour. 1 Peter 5:8.

The apostle Peters description of the devil as a roaring lion tells us what we are to expect from our enemy. The scripture shares with us the behavior patterns of the greatest unseen enemy of the human race. In Job 1:7; Satan was questioned by the Lord saying to him, "where do you come from"? Satan answered the Lord and said, "From roaming about the earth and walking around on it".

Our enemy is among us. He is the "king of beast" and he has a pride of lions (legions of demons) hunting for human prey. We have all seen and know what the lion does to their prey. I do not think we need any further details as to the method of consumption. The key word is that he devours his victim. All left-overs from the lions meal is cleaned up by scavengers.

2 Peter 2:1-22 gives us an explanation of the activities of the false prophets and teachers who are in our midst. Deceptions in all of its many forms are being introduced into every area of our society causing swift destruction to Gods creation. As you look around our planet earth, you see devastation in progress. Peter provides for us a persuasive argument concerning the influence of false teachers (2 Pet. 2:1-3); he gives analogies of the judgment of false teachers (2 Pet. 2:4-10a), he describes the character of false teachers (2 Pet. 2:10b-16) and he describes how false teachers "lead astray weaker people by enticing them back into a life of sin" (2 Pet. 2:17-22).

Our enemy operates in secret (Eph. 5:12), he does not want to be exposed. His method of attack is through deception. His weapon of choice are lies, his mystery of lawlessness is already at work (2 Thess. 2:7). Our enemy wants to gain control of our mind, he is a thief and his mission is to steal, kill and destroy (John 10:10). His other choice of weapon is the power of suggestion. He wants to plant thoughts into your mind and have you to believe that it was your thought (Matt. 15:19).

Perhaps our enemy's greatest deception is spreading the lie that he does not exist. These short essays on your enemies vicious thoughts are based on scriptural writing taken from the Holy Bible, God has recorded in his word the activities of the devil and how we are to resist (2 Tim. 3:16). Be alert, be on guard and be ready to fight the devil with the Word and make him flee from you. Consider these essays as a field manual, a battle plan of how the enemy launches his attacks against you. Remember, the Lord says, "My people perish for lack of knowledge".

Essay 0: The Angel of Music

I want your mind; I want to fill it up with my songs. Did you know that I was once in charge of the praise and worship ministry in heaven? I was the director of the ministry of melody, harmony, composition and song, all of which was tuned to perfection and almost as beautiful as I was. There was no other angel as gifted as I. I was the morning star, I was the greatest of all the angels and I had big plans for myself, I was on my way to the top and then suddenly I was thrown out of heaven, knocked down to the earth, It was fast, it was quick, a rapid descend from the presence of glory as Jesus saw me falling as fast as lightening from bliss to the dirt. I am now being referred to as the dragon, the ancient serpent, the devil and Satan, now leading the whole world amiss with those angels who were thrown out with me.[5]

I even tried to make Jesus an offer while He was on this earth, but he refused me and ordered me to leave him. Even so I am constantly trying to outwit you; I have numerous schemes to try on you, I would like to sift you as wheat. I am the god of this age; I control the minds of the unbelievers, to keep them in darkness and away from the light of the gospel. I have created music to make you lose your self-control; I prowl around like a roaring lion seeking to devour you.[6]

I was in Eden, Gods garden disguised as a serpent to take possession of what did not belong to me. Outside of the garden I was a spectacular specimen, I had the beauty of precious stones and gold, and when I moved, music was created, I was an anointed cherub and I was on the mountain of

---

5   Isa.14:11- 15 (NIV), Luke 10: 18 (NIV)
6   Matthew 4:10 (ISV), 2 Corinthians 2:11 (ESV), Luke 21: 31 (KJB), 2 Corinthians 4:4 (ASV), 1 Peter 5:8 (NIV)

God walking up and down in the midst of the stones of fire. I was perfect in my ways from the time that I was created, but I had some corruption issues, such heinousness things as injustice, wickedness, evil, vice, crime, various kinds of sin, things that God would not tolerate in his presence. With all of these things in me I was full of violence and was cast out as profane from the mountain of God and a death sentence was put upon me and my followers I was cut down to the ground, so I created a plan to continuously attack the nations of men. I say in my heart that I will exalt myself above the stars; I will become greater than God. In my heart I knew I was beautiful and bright, I was greater than the Seraphim, I was greater than the cherubim, I was greater than the Angels, I was Lucifer, the morning star.[7]

I love to set traps for believers, those who have good reputations, testimonies and above reproach, people who will let me fill their heart with deceits, this is a part of my earthly ministry. I enjoy getting humans to lie to the Holy Spirit. I am the king of the earth the angel from the bottomless pit, my name in Hebrew is Abaddon, and in Greek Apollyon; in Latin Exterminans. I am the personification of destruction. With me come my demons of obliteration, annihilation, devastation, demotion, ruin and damage to the hearts and soul of the human race. You passions of the earth will worship me. You will sing praises to me and you will do my bidding.[8]

---

7   Ezekiel 28:13-16 (NIV), Isaiah 14:11-14 (NIV)
8   1 Tim 3: 7 (BIBE), Acts 5: 3 (ASV), Rev. 9:11 (KJB), Rev. 9:11 (DRB)

The Thoughts of Essay 0

These are significant statements to think about, Selah

Review the scriptures and references in the footnotes for essay 0. Try to understand the thoughts of how you are being controlled through music. How does the melody of songs and poems rule your thoughts? How do these things power your emotions and feelings? Do the songs of the enemy inspire you to worship God, Do they motivate you to worship Jesus, and do they encourage you to worship the wisdom of the comforter?

Perhaps the songs of the enemy cause you to think of lust, desire, envy, covetousness, longing, yearning, hankering, hunger, thirst or itch? Does the enemy's song cause your heart to ache for someone or something? Do the lyrics produce the spirit of rebellion? Is there an inspiration to revolt; is there a spirit of revolution, mutiny, insurgence, agitation or insurrection?

Does the beat and rhyming of the music stimulate your desire to worship the kingdom of heaven or the kingdom of hell? Are you compelled to gyrate and dance in fleshly lust or spiritual worship?

Music was created by God as a form of worship. When you hear the melody, when you follow the tune, when you feel the harmony, when you begin to understand the composition and sing the song, ask yourself, who are you worshiping, what are you thinking of and does that piece of music bring joy or sadness. Does it introduce sin in your life or redemption? Is it holy or worldly?

We are reminded in scripture to be "addressing one another in psalms and hymns and spiritual songs, singing and making melody to the Lord with your heart". Eph. 5:19 (ESV)

There is still time, "You can change your form of worship".

"Let us come before him with thanksgiving and extol him with music and song". Psalm 95:2 (NIV)

Essay 1: The Enemy is a thief

I want what you have, just give me the opportunity and I will take it from you. I not only want what you need, I also want what you hope to get. I want it all. I am hungry and thirsty as I continuously roam about the earth and walking around on it looking for someone to devour.[9]

I am a roaring lion, I want to open my mouth and tear into your flesh, give me your precious life, do not worry about being brought with a price and do not concern yourself about honoring God with your body, give it to me so that I can dishonor it. You have a free choice, don't you? Why not indulge in sexual immorality, adultery, prostitution, homosexuality, what is wrong with becoming a drunkard, a slanderer, a swindler, an idolater, why worry about inheriting the kingdom of God and miss all the fun, just eat, drink, smoke, enjoy drugs. Your flesh will taste much better to me as I slowly consume you and gnaw on you bones.[10]

Do not forget that I am mighty and I do not turn away from anyone. Continue to ignore me so that I can tear you open and carry you off to my den where no one can rescue you. You will need the help of faith, the kind of faith that will subdue kingdoms, administer justice and obtain blessings of promise in order to close my mouth, but you are a fool and that is why I want your heart, it is the best piece of flesh, more suitable to my taste because it is corrupt, abominable and good for nothing, is it not written, there is none righteous, no not one, your mouth is full of cursing and bitterness. I wait for you as you walk through the earth, I look forward to striking you down to the place of fire and brimstone, and watch my predator allies seek to devastate you as you move about in your cities

---

9   Job 1:7 (NASB), 1 Peter 5:8 (NLT 2nd ed.).
10   Psalm 22:13 (NIV), 1 Cor. 6:20 (NIV), Eph. 6:7 (NIV), 1 Cor. 6:9-10 (NIV).

waiting for the opportunity to tear you to pieces. Your many transgressions and apostasies' will be my delight, so I will do to you as I have once done to Israel. I will hunt you like sheep, devour you and then gnaw on your wicked bones.[11]

Of course you have the power to strike back at me and of course you have protection and help to resist me and all of my evil plans for you and your love ones, but you cannot resist me because you do not believe that I exist. In fact you are so stupid that you do not believe in God and you absolutely reject His plan of salvation for you through His son Jesus. Does not the scripture warn you about affliction and anguish? Does not the scripture warn you about grief, distress, sadness and despair to those who have strayed from God! Destruction has come to you, because you have rebelled against the Lord! He longs to redeem you but you speak lies against Him.[12]

---

11 Proverbs 30:30 (Amp), Hosea 13:8 (AMP), Hosea 5:14 (AMP), Hebrews 11:33 (AMP), Psalm 14:1 (KJV), Rom. 3: 10-18 (KJV), Rom. 3: 14 (KJV), Jeremiah 5:6 (ESV), Jeremiah 50: 17 (AMP).
12 Ps 91 (NLT), John 3:16 (ESV), Hosea 7:13 (NIV).

The Thoughts of Essay 1

These are important statements to think about, Selah

Review the scriptures and references in the footnotes for essay 1. Try to understand and think of how you are being robbed by the thief. How does his stealing from you rule your thoughts? Hosea 4:2 says "There is only cursing, lying and murder, stealing and adultery; they break all bounds, and bloodshed follows bloodshed". How do these things influence your emotions and feelings? Do the actions of the enemy anger you? Do the plans of your adversary cause you annoyance, irritation, fury, rage, antagonism or resentment?

Your opponent wants all of what God has given to you. Your foe wants your life. He wants your existence. Your being, your time, living, days, years and demise he will gladly take from you. He will stop at nothing and will leave you with nothing.

Your enemy wants your God given freedom. He desires to take away your liberty, autonomy, self-determination, independence, choice, sovereignty and free will. Your life is precious to God, it is so precious that He sent His Son to redeem you and bring you into eternal life. Our antagonist is a deadly nemesis. He wants you to dishonor your body; he wants you to indulge in sexual deviations and destructive eating and drinking habits, He wants you to develop addictions and mutilate the beautiful body the Lord has given you.

We are reminded in scripture to resist. The scripture warns us to "Submit yourselves therefore to God. Resist the devil, and he will flee from you." James 4:7 (KJV)

We are reminded in scripture to fight back. The scripture says "Resist him, standing firm in the faith, because you know that your brothers throughout the world are undergoing the same kind of sufferings" 1 Peter 5:9 (NIV).

Essay 2: I am Looking, Watching & Waiting for Opportunities

I am going to make you powerful and rich; I want you to forget all about God, do not acknowledge Him. Who is this God anyway? Have you seen Him? Does He talk to you? You have anything to gain by praying to what you cannot see, you certainly won't profit from knowing Him, come and join us, throw your lot in with us, you have heard of us before. We are deception.[13]

Forget about wisdom, don't waste your time on her, she can't protect you, neither can her two companions, discretion and understanding; we enjoy deceiving those who are perishing. We are setting traps to get you, we are seeking to ruin you, and all day long we think of you being caught in the many snares designed especially for you, we want to give you the whole world, but in exchange we want your life, we want your soul. [14]

There is a large group of us wicked spirits, we are also called legion, and we would like to inhabit you, take over your life and control you. You could become a part of the wicked generation and just lay back and enjoy a season of sin. We want you to avoid Jesus, we do not want you to come to your right mind and miss all the fun we have planned for you. We will introduce you to the new loves of your life, the delight of drinking, feasting and sleeping. You will have pleasure and luxury and be rich, this is what we have plan for you, you can be powerful. Just think about it, plenty of wine and beer, mixed drinks and you can gorge yourself on fine meats and

---

13 John 6:46 (AKJV), John 4:24 (KJB), 1 John 4:16 (ISV), Psalm 4:6 (NIV), Prov. 2:11 (NIV), 2 Thess. 2:10 (NIV), Psalm 38:12 (ASV), Mat 16:26 (NASB)
14 Jer. 5:27 (GWT), Jer. 9:6 (ESV), Job 21:15 (NIV), Job 34:9 (NASB),

all kinds of women and men and children will make themselves available to you.[15]

Forget about Godly wisdom, accept our wisdom, it is worldly, self-centered and very enjoyable, reject Gods free gift of eternal life and accept our free gift to you, death.[16]

---

15 Mark 5:9 (BIBE), Matt 12:45 (NIV), Mark 5:8 (NIV), Mark 5:15 (NIV), Prov. 23:21 (BIBE), Prov. 21:17 (NLT), Prov. 6:11 (NIV), Prov. 20:1 (NIV), Isa. 5:22 (NIV), Prov. 23:20 (NIV), Prov. 6:26 (NIV)
16 James 3:15 (GWT), Rom. 6:23 (ESV)

The Thoughts of Essay 2

These are vital statements to think about, Selah

Review the scriptures and references in the footnotes for essay 2. Try to understand the thoughts of how you are being deceived by the enemy. How does his promise of power and riches appeal to you? How do these potential possibilities rule your thoughts? 1 John 2:16 (NIV) says "For everything in the world--the cravings of sinful man, the lust of his eyes and the boasting of what he has and does--comes not from the Father". How do these things influence your emotions and feelings? Do the deceptions of the enemy appeal to you? Or are you wise to the devils trickery. His promises are nothing but a sham, he is a fraud. Your enemy is self-centered, self-absorbed, self-seeking and egotistic.

The enemy is a defeated foe. His greatest desire is to be God and he will try to be like God. He wants us to worship him as God even though he can never be God. He is a false god. The god of this world is deceptive, a phony and a murder.

The devil cannot offer you anything because he does not have anything good to give. All that he has was stolen. He wants to offer to you what he stole from you, He is a thief, a counterfeit and deceitful in all that he does. He cannot give you true power and riches. He can only pretend to give you what he stole and then take it back.

We are reminded in scripture about deception. The prophet says, "But you have planted wickedness, you have reaped evil, you have eaten the fruit of deception, because you have depended on your own strength and on your many warriors". Hosea 10:13 (NIV)

We are reminded in scripture in the book of Job. The scripture says "Yet they say to God, 'Leave us alone! We have no desire to know your ways. Job 21:14 (NIV)

Essay 3: The Relentless & Persistent Hunter

I am hunting you, I am putting pressure on you, I want to confront you, I am your enemy. I want to separate you from the love of Christ, I am the "who" the bible talks about, I am the "what" that will try to separate you from the love of Father God. I want to cause you pain and sorrow; I encourage you to do evil especially those of you who have been chosen, does not His word say that "He will punish you for all your sins", do not worry about that. I have other plans for you.[17]

However, I will pursue you, me and my painted dogs, we will run after you, we will separate the weak from among you, we will run you down, we will kill you and consume your flesh, like a disease we will destroy you slowly, but do not be concerned about that, just listen to me my children, I am your father, do what I tell you and you will have pleasure and you will fulfill your desires, I speak the truth, you belong to me, forget about doing what is right, I will tell you what to do, forget about what the Lord says, do not try to contain me, and do not try to contain yourself, Leave the straightway and follow the wide way to riches, follow the path of Balaam for profit, enjoy the pleasures of immorality, make your body feel good, do not worry about the warnings of sexual depravity, these are the acts of the normal human being.[18]

There is nothing wrong with having a good appetite, I influenced Eglon king of Moab and he became a very big man in his day, so go your own way and be all that you can. I am the destroyer, I will kill you, my dogs will drag you away and the beasts will devour you. My dogs ate the flesh

---

17 Rom 8:35 (ESV), Rom 8: 35 (GWT), Rom 2:9 (AKJV), Amos 3:2 (D-RB)
18 Association of Zoos & Aquariums, John 8:44 (NASB), 2 Peter 2:15 (NIV), Jude 1:11 (NLT), Numbers 25:1-16 (NIV), 1 Cor. 6:18 (BIBE), Gal. 5:19 (NIV)

of Jezebel, that pretty, murderous idol worshiping beauty and they expelled her from their stomachs as dung. Do not worry about your family, eat your own bread, look after yourself, it is the right thing to do. Do not listen to those who tell you to watch out for the dogs, it is said that they are your best friend, it has also been said that I love falsehood, but do not burden yourself with that, I love magic, sexual wickedness, murder and such, small issues of no consequence.[19]

I am the one who influence Nimrod and Esau to become depraved hunters. Nimrod was the first mighty warrior on earth a hunter of men, and Esau a hunter of wild game who showed contempt for his God given birth right and gave it up for a meal of bread and stew, I am the painted dog. I look for and hunt for victims. I watch for easy prey. The ungodly are my choice; they are profane, hypocritical, crude and abusive. They are malicious jesters who mock and deceive. These are my dogs, enemies of the righteous, they open their mouths wide against the Lords anointed; they scoff and gnash their teeth and say, "We have swallowed her up. This is the day we have waited for; we have lived to see it." Chase them, devour them all. I will also go after the righteous, all my demons will band together and we will go after those who have done no wrong. My demons will conspire, they will lurk, and they watch every step, eager to take your life.[20]

---

19 2 Kin. 9:37 (NIV), 2 Kin. 9:36 (NIV), Isa. 56:11 (NIV), Jer. 15:3 (NIV), Matt. 15:26 (NIV), Phil. 3:2 (NIV), Rev. 22:15 (NIV), Jude 1:3-16

20 Gen. 10:9 (NIV), Gen. 25:27 (NIV), Gen. 10:8 (NLT), Gen. 25:34 (NLT), Ps. 35:16 (NIV), Lam. 2:16 (NIV), Ps. 94:21 (BIBE).

The Thoughts of Essay 3

Very significant statements "Think on Them", Selah

Review the scriptures and references in the footnotes for essay 3. Try to understand the thoughts of how you are being hunted; think about the relentless persistent pursuit of the enemy. His determination to steal your life, his resolve to kill you and all that belongs to you, his depth of thoughts to destroy your happiness.

You are being chased by a pack of dogs that are bonded together in the seeds of bitterness, resentment, anger, hostility, cynicism and indignation. The love of God for you has put a bitter taste in the mouths of these beleaguers. They want to taste the sweetness of innocence, they want to taste the tartness of stupidity, and they look forward to gulping the sour taste of those who ignore the love of God and his anointed.

There is no safety for those who refuse the love of the Father, there is no protection for those who refuse to be rescued by the Son of the Father, the Lord Jesus, and there is no comfort for those who depress the Holy Spirit.

You are living on borrowed time. The dogs are in hot pursuit of your life. They desire your soul. They will run after you until you drop from exhaustion. As you lay there defenseless they will begin to consume you, you are overwhelm by these mongrels, and they are obsessed with your destruction. You are being gobbled up, you are being demolished.

They have successfully hounded you, they have successfully stalked you. The hunt is over. You have died in your sins. There is no hope for you. Your enemy, your father, the devil has you in his belly and there you will rot and waste away to be expelled as manure. Your soul will live forever in the pit and in that place; the demons and the worm that never dies will torment you for eternity.

There is still time, "You can escape this madness".

"I tell you the truth, whoever accepts anyone I send accepts me; and whoever accepts me accept the one who sent me." John 13:20 (NIV)

Essay 4: That dragon, that serpent, that devil, Satan

I am the dragon, also known as the old serpent, many times referred to as the devil, I have many titles, and one of my favorites is that of being referred to as the accuser "Satan". I have a reputation for being crafty. Many in God's creation are not smart enough to identify my deceitful schemes. I have used the same trick I used on Eve in the garden which led to Adam and Eves fall. It was very effective and I am still using it today. From the time that I and my angels were kicked out of heaven we have been using the same methods to lead the whole world astray.[21]

I have a number of deception tactics that I use on those who are perishing; these are the human souls who reject the love and truth of the Word. These are those who delight themselves in wickedness and have become marked for condemnation, these are the ones who refuse the protection of wisdom; they believe that the teaching of the cross is foolishness; these are the souls who have the spirit of Cain and the disposition of Cain's decedents. God's creation does not realize that I am the god of this world and that I can manipulate the minds of all unbelievers by deception. [22]

If I could I would try to deceive the very elect through my false ministers with signs and wonders and make them useless in their kingdom building for Christ. I have cultivated a wicked plan to feed the whole human race with the fruit of lies and deceptions making then think they can save their nations through war. I have manipulated all of mankind, especially those

---

21 Rev. 20: 2 (NIV), Gen. 3:1 (NASB), 2 Cor. 11:3 (NIV), 2 Tim. 2:15 (NIV). Gen. 4:6-21 (NSAB).

22 2 Th. 2:10 (NLT), 2 Th. 2:12 (NIV), Pr. 4:6 (NIV), 1 Cor. 1:18 (NIV), 2 Cor. 4:4 (NLT), Jer. 9:6 (ASV),

who deny God, and also those who reject the one who He has sent to die for their sins. You are all fools and ridiculers and marked for punishment, and when I am finally sent to the lake of fire made for me and my angels, I will gladly share it with you, and I will torment you for all eternity. All of us rebels will be in the lake together including death and hades; other eternal guess will be the false prophet and the beast, and a whole host of souls who hated the LORD, all crying and screaming in torment forever.[23]

I am the fraudster; I have cheated, swindled and lied. I have done all the things I needed to do to fool Gods creation, and now, there are many who are not living guiltless lives, they ignore God, they curse, they murder, they speak wicked words, they kill their children, husbands and wives despise each other, misery and ruin is spreading, leadership is corrupt, there is no peace. They have no clue that it is me who is the master mind of all the world's problems, not any of them understand, and because of their lack of knowledge I will destroy them, I will strike them like a dragon, unseen, quite, fast and deadly. If your name is not written in the Lambs book of life, your soul belongs to me.[24]

23 Matt. 24:22-24 (ASV), Hos. 10:13 (ESV), Pr. 19:29 (ESV), Rev. 20:14 (ASV), Rev. 20:10 (NIV), Psalm 81:15 (NASB)
24 Rom. 3:10-19 (NIV), Hosea 4:6 (NIV), Rev. 20:15 (ISB)

The Thoughts of Essay 4

These are significant statements "Think on them", Selah

Review the scripture and references in the footnote for essay 4. Try to understand the thoughts of the enemy. How does he accomplish the role of an accuser? How is he able to hide himself from you? How is he able to cause destruction and misery in the world and avoid being liable. How is it that God gets blamed for all of the evil in the world and not the devil?

"So Satan left the LORD's presence, and he struck Job with terrible boils from head to foot", Job 2:7 (NLT). The enemy wants to accuse you of doing wrong. He is constantly testing you. He is persistently trying to get you to curse God for your trials and tribulations. He relentlessly comes after you. He tempts you and then exposes your sin. "For there is nothing hidden that will not be disclosed, and nothing concealed that will not be known or brought out into the open. Luke 8:17 (NIV).

Are you living in honesty? Do you have honor, do you live in truthfulness? Do you have veracity? Scripture says; "The man of integrity walks securely, but he who takes crooked paths will be found out". Proverbs 10:9 (NIV). Our enemy is still using the same old tricks, the same tricks he use in centuries past.

There is still time, expose him, you may not be able to see him but you can see the evidence of his presence in the world and in your society. "But His hatred is deceitfully hidden, but his wickedness will be revealed to the community", Prov. 26:26 (GWT).

Do not be foolish choose life. 1 John 5:12 (NIV)

Essay 5: The Strongman

I am the strong man, without Gods authority you cannot enter my house and take back what I stole from you. I encouraged the spirit of the ancient Canaanites who were living among the Jews, I enjoyed watching them become an economic nuisance to Gods people; I will always be in the midst of the human family plotting to steal, kill and destroy. I want to keep you in need; I want to keep you in poverty, I want to promote shortages, create famine, initiate deprivation and hold back your wealth. I control the spirit of power and greed; I want it all and leave you with nothing. I want your family, especially your children; I have placed the spirit of Moloch among you. Reject your children and abort them, reject your responsibility as a parent and leave them unprotected, why be inconvenienced, turn away from your children and give them to me.[25]

I love rebellious people; I love deceitful children, children who are not willing to follow the LORD's instruction, I love to see children disobey their parents and make their own decisions; there are plenty of drugs, plenty of sex, tobacco, alcohol and parties. Be a run away from home, do your own thing and discover life without rules. I also enjoy seeing children suffering from famine, from war and watching them starve, yes give me your children so that I can terminate them. I want people to be lovers of their own selves, be all that they want to be, be arrogant, abusive and ungrateful, take charge of your life and take what you want.[26]

Fathers do not have time for their children, I love to manipulate them to exasperate their children, to make them bitter and discouraged. Fathers,

---

25 Mark 3:27 (NIV), John 10:10 (NIV), Leviticus 20:2 (GWT), Jeremiah 18:21 (ASV), (Enlow, 2008, Chapter 4), (Phillips, 2010, Chapter 3)
26 Isa.30:9 (NIV), Eph. 6:1 (NLT), Jer. 18:21 (ESV), 2 Tim. 3:2 (ISV)

who can be influenced to force their whole family to worship the queen of heaven, Fathers who will force their families to try to please God in the wrong manner, a way that leads to death. I love to manipulate the wives to be quarrelsome, contentious and brawling. There is nothing better than watching a disgraceful wife causing decay to her man's bones. I like jealousy, I want to see cancer in the bones of man, I want to see envy rot the bones of women, and I do not want to see any healthy bodies. I am he who eats peoples flesh, break their bones in pieces and throw them into the pot to devour.[27]

Wives do not have time to be mothers of children, why should they submit to their husbands, they have their own careers, who cares about raising children and doing good deeds.[28]

---

27 Col. 3:21 (NIV), Eph. 6:4 (NIV), Jer. 7:18 (NASB), Prov. 14:12 (NIV), Prov. 12:4 (NIV), Prov. 14:30 (NIV), Micah 3:2 (NIV)
28 Col. 3:18 (NIV), 1 Tim. 5:10 (NIV)

The Thoughts of Essay 5

Noteworthy statement's to think about, Selah

Review the scriptures and references in the footnotes for essay 5. Try to understand the thoughts of the enemy concerning how he is attacking you. Ask yourself the following questions. Do you know how to fight back? Do you have the authority to fight back? Do you have the authority to retake what you have lost? Do you have the spiritual knowledge to stand against evil?

Do you know how to intercede for and plan to rescue the perishing, the dying, the poor, and the innocent? Have you studied the great commission? Have you seriously put an effort into following Jesus Command? Review Matthew 28:19-20.

Are you following the disciple's commission? Review Mark 16:15-18. Did not Jesus say "you are my disciples", did He not say "Love one another", John 13:35.

You have power, Acts 1:8. Go and do the Acts of the Apostles. Preach, teach, and reclaim the backslidden. Review what Luke said in Luke 24:45-49. If you are a disciple of Jesus, you have been clothed with power from on high. Go on the offensive, use the authority given to you; you have power, use it!

Essay 6: The Wolf Man

You are my prey, we will deal with you in the same manner as with Benjamin, in the morning we will devour you and in the evening we will be dividing the spoils. We will hunt you down; we will chase you and wear you out. We will stay in hot pursuit of you until we catch you and then we will rip you to pieces. I am the prince in the midst of wolves, we love the shedding of blood, we love destroying lives and we will do all we can to get dishonest gain from you and your love ones. [29]

I know you very well, you refuse to listen, you refuse to repent, and you do not know the ways of the Lord, so come to me, give yourself to me so that I can have my demons strike you down, devastate you and your families and lay in wait for you as you leave your cities and then attack, we love the taste of your transgressions and the great smell of your apostasies. We love all of those who are in authority, those who do not know the Holy One. We roar like lions coming after the prey, we love the wicked judges and will consume you and leave nothing of you till tomorrow because we will devour all of your flesh. [30]

We are persecution, and we are continuously coming for you, you are like sheep in the midst of wolves, the only thing that can save you is being wise as serpents and innocent as doves, but you are stupid and will not pay attention to the WAY. We are always watching out for the anointed ones, they are lambs among us wolves, we are waiting for you to stray from the TRUTH. We are always looking for the minister or teacher who is guiding a group of people to sin and leave the flock and run when he sees us so that we can snatch and scatter the lambs. The guide is nothing

---

29 Gen 49:27 (NIV), Ezekiel 22:27 (ESV)
30 Jeremiah 5:6 (ESV), Zephaniah 3:3 (ESV)

but a hired hand and cares nothing for the sheep because the LIFE is not in him. [31]

I know that the day is coming when my cavernous nature will be removed and that there will be peace on earth. I know that the day is coming when we shall be subdued by the Lord, but until then we will continue to steal, kill and destroy as many as we can. I will come among you and spare no one I will influence many of you to speak twisted things and draw you to destruction. I have many false prophets dressed in disguised who are inwardly ravening Casanovas. Although we are wolves, we are members of the family of dogs; we are man's best friend. Give us what is sacred, give us what is holy, we have mighty appetites, we never have enough to eat, we love to prowl, we are vicious during the night. Your watchmen are blind and they lack knowledge, they are Stupid fools, they do not have the ability to warn, they cannot bark, they lie around and dream. While the watchmen sleep we mutilate all flesh.[32]

---

31 Matt 10:16 (ESV), John 10:12 (ESV), Luke 10:3 (ESV)
32 Isaiah 11:6 (NIV), Isaiah 65:25 (NIV), Acts 20:29 (ESV), Matt. 7:16, 7:6 (NIV), Isaiah 56:11 (NIV), Ps. 59:6 (NIV), Isa 56:10 (NIV), Phil, 3:2 (NIV).

The Thoughts in Essay 6

Very expressive declarations to think about, Selah

Review the scriptures and references in the footnotes for essay 6. Try to comprehend the thoughts of the enemy and how you are considered to be prey. You are the quarry. All those who do not know Christ as Lord and Savior are targeted for damnation, they are victims, they are nothing but wild game being hunted and then slaughtered. All those who know Christ as Lord and Savior are targets for harassment "Every believer is subject to temptation, deception, oppression, and strongholds", (Phillips, 2010, Chapter 3).

Do you listen? What does Matthew 13:18 say? Do you understand? Mark 4:13. Are you listening?

Who is persecuting you? Do you know who is hounding you day and night, who is baiting and tormenting you? What is the cause of all of this badgering? Could it be an unclean spirit? Could it be a hidden enemy? The one who is stealth, the one who is camouflage as unseen and strikes at your unsuspecting nature.

It is your deadly enemy who preaches unsound doctrine; he is after you day and night. 1 Tim. 1:10.

"Resist" (James 4:7)

Essay 7: Fresh Meat

There is nothing better than fresh meat. Look what I did to Adam and Eve my very first victims. I used my cunning to deceive them. I made them doubt what the Lord had said to them; I made them rebel against the creator. It was so easy, in reality, they both were duped by me and I got them kicked out of the garden. Of course they blamed me for their stupidity and the Lord has placed a curse on me, but the trap has been set to deceive the whole human race in the same manner I am doing at this very moment. The days are coming when I will be bound up for a time, but I will be released again to continue my deception. [33]

I am Satan, I tried to temp the Lord in the wilderness, three times I tried to get Him, but His power was too strong, He was weak after 40 days of fasting but He still rejected me, demonstrating to all His followers to come on how to defeat me. I am the prince of devils; I am a constant enemy of God and His anointed. I hate the truth, I love to lie and I love cruelty, I love evil. I have great power in this world; I take men captive and devour them. I know that you Christians are warned about my tricks and I know that you are taught to resist me, but do not forget I have the power of death you cannot continue to ignore my deceits, you cannot continue to resist me, I am the executioner. [34]

I am the prince of the power of the air; I have control over all of you disobedient people, I am the god of this world, yes, it is me the ancient one with all of my demons, and we don't want you to see the LIGHT, I am the ruler of this world and I want your soul. But I do not want to move

---

33 Gen. 3:1-4 (ESV), Gen. 3:13-14 (ESV), 2 Cor. 11:3 (ESV), Rev. 20:2-3 (ESV)
34 Matt. 4:1-11 (ESV), Matt. 12:24 (ESV), 1 Pet. 5:8 (NIV), 2 Tim. 2:26 (ESV), 2 Cor. 2:11 (ESV), James 4:7 (ESV)

too quickly in achieving my plans. I want to condition your mind. My servant Beelzebub, lord of the flies, the master of lies, and creator of false teachings will school you on such subjects as pride, boasting, haughtiness, humanism, liberalism, rationalism and atheism. [35]

I want to transform your thinking; I want control of your thoughts, I want to put emphases on your understanding of truth, you need to be rational and display critical thinking. I Beelzebub will control your education, we demons will help develop your left brain hemisphere, and we want control of the mountains of God. [36]

---

35 Eph. 2:1-2 (ESV), 2 Cor. 4:4 (ESV), Rev. 12: 9 (ESV), Rev. 20:2 (ESV), John 12:31, 14:30 (ESV), (Enlow, 2008, Chapter 7), Acts 20:30 (ESV), 2 Pt. 2:1 (ESV), 2 Cor. 11:27 (ESV)
36 (Taylor, 2004, Chapter 6), (Enlow, 2008, Chapter 7)

The Thoughts in Essay 7

Dramatic thoughts of the enemy, how does the enemy see us? Selah

We are seen as prey, a hunted victim that can be baited. We can be drawn into sin; we are lured into entanglements, enticed and pulled in by deceitful temptations. There are many witnesses watching what is going on. "Put off your old self, who is being corrupted by its deceitful desires". Think about things that are excellent and worthy of praise.

Review and study the scriptures in the footnotes of essay 7. Review the references as well.

Our enemy wants to provoke, goad, tease and taunt you. He shows you the carrot and then draws you in for the slaughter. The carrot of sin is the attraction, but as you reach for it, he attacks. Your hand is caught before you take it and then the torment begins.

How long will you be a prey? How long will you be a target? It is better to be victorious through Christ Jesus than a victim at the hands of your sworn enemy?

Please review Hebrews 12:1, Ephesians 4:22, Philippians 4:8. Think about it, Act on it, Do it.

Essay 8: Offering your Children

I want your Children, give them to me for sacrifice, give them to me so that I can make them pass through the fires of abortion, incest, prostitution, abuse, torture, abandonment, neglect and famine. Let me put them through the fires of Moloch, where they can do drugs and join gangs, to murder and commit all sorts of mayhem. If they get bored, there is always suicide. Think about it? [37]

I will put them on the path of the ancient Canaanite's, on the corridor that will lead them to steal, kill, and destroy, I want them to be disobedient. I want them to reject knowledge and be destroyed. I want to frustrate them and watch them curse their fathers and bless not their mothers, I want to see them running around in the darkness. No light, nothing but the blackness.[38]

I have numerous schemes and can outwit all humans, including the very elect, I am the god of this world, I have blinded the minds of the unbelievers, they know nothing of the light of the gospel and they are ignorant of the glory of Jesus who is the image of God. I will get them to do what I tried to get Job to do; I will get them to curse God to His face. Let me have control of your children and I will influence them to kill widows and foreigners and murder orphans. Give me control of the minds of the youth so that they can focus on human nature, they should be focusing on their sinful nature fulfilling my goals of man's destruction, I want them all with me, I want them to have their portion in the lake of

---

37   Lev.18:21 (GWT), Jer.32:35(NLT)
38   Prov. 16:25 (NLT), CARM, Jer. 7:9-10 (NIV), Hos. 4:6 (KJB), Prov. 30:11 (ASV), Prov. 20:20 (ERV)

fire and brimstone, which is the second death. The earth is mine, I do not want to share it or give it up, and it belongs to me. [39]

I want absolute control of your children's minds; I want them to do detestable things, I want to educate them on the arts of perversion, there will be no more healthy teaching. I do not want them to learn about the kingdom of God. My deceptions are much better for them; I have plans to promote wickedness. Your children shall not be taught sound doctrine; they shall become fornicators, kidnappers, liars, immoral persons, homosexuals. They shall learn of these things and practice them; they shall be acting as my puppets, under my influence never knowing that they are being manipulated by the enemy of God, I exist, I am in your mist, and I will control you, I AM Satan, the god of this world. [40]

---

39   2 Cor. 2:11 (ESV), Anderson (2000), 2 Cor. 4:4 (ESV), Ps. 96:6 (NLT), Romans 8:6 (ISV), Galatians 6:8 (NIV), Rev. 21:8 (AKJV)
40   Lev. 20:13 (ESV), Rom. 1:27 (NIV), 1 Tim. 1:10 (ISV), 1 Cor. 6:9 (NIV), Sears & Osten (2003)

The Thoughts of Essay 8

Your enemy's thoughts concerning your children

Our enemy has always desired our children. There have always been depraved demonic thoughts about the mistreatment and destruction of the innocent. The bible mentions the horrors of the sacrifices to the god of Moloch, Leviticus 18:21, Leviticus 20:2.

Jeremiah has written about the disgusting acts administered to children in Jeremiah 7:31 and Jeremiah 19:4.

What does the prophet have to say about the sacrifice of the innocent in Ezekiel? Look at Ezekiel 20:30-31 and Ezekiel 23:37.

Review the footnotes of essay 8, study, mediate on them.

Is our society still doing the same things? Is our society still worshiping the god of Moloch and all of the demonic forces for the sake of convenience? Has abortion become the new demon of this world, which is the same demon of the old world? Have we developed reasons to terminate the unborn, have we established reasons to end life? Do we abandon our children? Do we quit on them? Do we call off birth? Do we call a halt to reproducing life? Do we stop midstream Gods command to replenish the earth?

Do we break off living and except death? Our existence is a problem for the enemy. Death to human life is his solution. Think about these things and choose life, Deuteronomy 30:19.

Essay 9: Sudden Death

I will overtake you, suddenly, without warning; I will pull you into the pit. All humans' are like grass. They pass away like a wild flower. Yes, you of little faith, you are here today and tomorrow you will be thrown into the fire. You are not wise; you do not accept the wisdom from the comforter. You fear mortal men and they are all nothing but grass. All of men's glory is like the grass of the field. You are nothing but a phantom; you are very busy moving about the earth, all of your hard work is vanity and your wealth will eventually come to me. You will spring up like a flower, but you will not endure.[41]

You are a man, you are like a breath, and your days are like a fleeting shadow, you will die. You are as wicked as I am, things will not go well with you, and does not the scripture say that you are like your father, I am your father and your days are numbered. You are like green plants that soon die away. You will perish away forever like your own dung. It is appointed for you to die once and after that comes your judgment. Does not the scripture say "By the sweat of your brow you will have food to eat until you return to the ground from which you were made? For you were made from dust, and to dust you will return". [42]

Does not the scripture say again "and the dust returns to the ground it came from, and the spirit returns to God who gave it". But you are a sinner, all of you have sinned and fall short of the glory of God. Your soul is mine, it belongs to me, and have you not read "For the wages of sin is death". I

---

41   1 Peter 1:24 (ISV), James 1:10 (NIV), Matt. 6:30 (NIV), Isa. 51:12 (NIV), Isa. 40:6 (NIV), Ps. 39:6 (NIV), Job 14:2 (NIV)
42   Ps. 144:4 (NIV), Eccles. 8:13 (NIV), Ps. 37:2 (NIV), Job 20:7 (NIV), Eccles. 9:1-6 (ESV), Gen. 3:19 (NLT),

shall take your soul to hell when you die. "There is not a righteous man on earth who does what is right and never sins". God is angry with you because of your sins, and I will take you captive to my land, a land where it is hot, a land where there is pain and suffering, a land where the screams are eternal and you have no rest. You will be in a land where you can smell the smoke of torment, a land of fire and brimstone, where the worm never dies and the fire is never quenched, you shall be in everlasting punishment, all of you unrighteous souls, except the righteous, they shall escape hell, and move on into eternal life with Jesus.[43]

But know for sure that the entire unrighteous are fools, what does the scripture say? "The fool has said in his heart, there is no God. They are corrupt, they have done abominable works, there is none that does good". If you have not given your heart to Jesus, you belong to me, the Lord sees your wickedness and he sees your inclinations, He knows your thoughts, you are evil, you are of your father, the "devil", you belong to me. [44]

---

43 Eccles. 12:7 (NIV), Rom. 3:23 (NIV), Rom. 6:23 (NIV), Eccles. 7:20 (NIV), 1 Kings 8:46 (NIV), Rev. 14:11 (NIV), Rev. 20:10 (NIV), Mark 9:48 (NIV), Matt. 25:46 (NIV),
44 Ps. 14:1 (AKJV), Gen. 6:4 (NIV), Gen. 6:5 (NIV), John 8:44 (NIV)

The Thoughts of Essay 9

Our enemy reveals his feelings about death. What are your thoughts, Selah?

Death and Destruction are never satisfied, and neither are the eyes of man, Proverbs 27:20.

Have the gates of death been shown to you? Have you seen the gates of the shadow of death? Job 38:17.

Death is naked before God; Destruction lies uncovered. Job 26:6.

For death has come up through our windows; It has entered our palaces To cut off the children from the streets, The young men from the town squares. Jeremiah 9:21.

He brought up against them the king of the Babylonians, who killed their young men with the sword in the sanctuary, and spared neither young man nor young woman, old man or aged. God handed all of them over to Nebuchadnezzar. 2 Chronicles 36:17.

Even youths grow tired and weary, and young men stumble and fall; Isaiah 40:30.

So give their children over to famine; hand them over to the power of the sword. Let their wives be made childless and widows; let their men be put to death, their young men slain by the sword in battle. Jeremiah 18:21.

Yet you refuse to come to me to have life. John 5:40.

Meditate on these scriptures; think about he who has the keys to death and the one who has the keys to eternal life. "Whoever believes in the Son has eternal life, but whoever rejects the Son will not see life, for God's wrath remains on him." John 3:36.

Essay 10: Give me the two things that God gave you!

Give me your mind; I want to see your sinful nature take control. Sin does not worry about being under the authority of God, your free will won't allow it, and your sinful nature won't permit it. I want to place thoughts in your mind, but I want you to think it is your own thoughts. I want you to become a friend of the world; I want you to do the things that the world does. I know you very well, you do not love the Lord your God with all your heart, with all your soul and with your entire mind, and with all your strength. You cannot possibly love God because you have a hostile mind and you will not submit to Him. I have the ability to deceive the whole world. I have a liar's nature and I am the father of lies, but I do not want you to know about it.[45]

Give me your heart. I love the heart because it is deceitful, it is desperately wicked. The word of God says "For from within, out of men's hearts, come evil thoughts, sexual immorality, theft, murder, adultery". That is why I want to keep control of the hearts of mankind. The human heart is full of greed, malice, deceit, lewdness, envy, slander, arrogance and folly. The scripture continues to discuss all of the traits of the hearts of men, "This is the evil in everything that happens under the sun: The same destiny overtakes all. The hearts of men, moreover, are full of evil and there is madness in their hearts while they live, and afterward they join the dead". In the end you will come to me.[46]

I am Apollyon, I am destruction, and I am the one who destroys. I control the mountain of media, I despise virtue, I control the rational mind, and

---

45   Rom. 8:6 (NIV), Rom. 8:7 (GWT), Anderson (2000), James 4:4 (NIV), Mark
     12:30 (NIV), Rev. 12:9 (NIV), John 8:44 (NIV)
46   Jer. 17:9 (KJB), Mark 7:21- 22 (NIV), Eccels. 9:3 (NIV)

I fill the air with liberalism, bad news, terrorism, fear, all the things that bring danger and damage. I control the airwaves, all of your media outlets are under my control. Fear and terror are my specialty and I work on the hearts and minds of God's creation. Man knows about God but he refuses to glorify Him and neither will they thank Him. Men are fools and their hearts are full of darkness. My goal is to promote humanism and reduce in importance any and all acknowledgement of God. Men play into my hands because they hear the words of God but do not put it into practice.[47]

I, the god of this world have blinded the minds of the unbelievers, they cannot see the light. They are all walking according to the course of this world. It is me, the prince of the power of the air, the spirit that controls them. They all have carnal minds, they belong to me.[48]

---

47 Rev. 9 (ESV), Enlow (2008), Phil. 4:8 (ESV), Rom. 1:21 (NIV), James 1:22 (ISV)

48 2 Cor. 4:4 (AKJV), Eph. 2:2 (AKJV), Rom. 8:7 (AKJV)

The Thoughts of Essay 10

Your enemy wants your mind and heart. What are your opinions? Selah

What does the scripture say about your thoughts?
Ephesians 2:3.

What does the scripture say about your heart?
Romans 1:24.

What does the scripture say about your mind?
Colossians 1:21

Think about how you use to live and how you followed the ways of this world?
Ephesians 2:2.

Are you alert? Do you have self-control?
1 Thessalonians 5:6.

Review the footnotes of essay 10 and the references.
What are you thinking about? Are you living by the Spirit?

This should be your captivating thought. "So I say, live by the Spirit, and you will not gratify the desires of the sinful nature". Galatians 5:16

Essay 11: I Love to Teach and Seduce

I want you to be lovers of human pleasure more than lovers of God. I want to teach you the art of treason, to be prepared and ready to do anything. I want you to be inflated with pride and to be full of self-conceit. You must be principled and breathe out arrogance, and show full love for pleasure. I am your enemy, I will expose you to betrayal, and I will expose you to denying the truth and teach you how to betray with a kiss.[49]

I have many false prophets in the world, and they will deceive many of you, you shall all fall away from the truth. I will cause you to be a destroyer, I will cause you to betray. I am full of signs and wonders with wicked deceptions for those who perish, especially prepared for those who love not the truth. I have many seducing spirits proclaiming the doctrines of demons causing many to leave the faith and believe the lie. I have a house for you, a place where you can stay for a while and have your fill of pleasure. All the foolish men and women go down this path, a path that leads to the chambers of death.[50]

I have led many down that path, the small and the great, the rich and the poor, mighty leaders and warriors, even the religious and the educators, all of them sinful men and women. They were all surprised when they found out what awaits them. The scripture says, "Her feet go down to death; her steps lead straight to the grave". Do you not know that "Outside are the dogs, those who practice magic arts, the sexually immoral, the murderers, the idolaters and everyone who loves and practices falsehood"? In the

---

49 Rev. 2:20 (ESV), 2 Tim. 3:4 (NIV), Enlow (2008), Biblos.com (2004-2011), Luke 22:4 (NIV), Luke 22:48 (AKJV)

50 Matt. 24:11 (NIV), Matt. 11:6 (NIV), Isa. 33:1 (ESV), 2 Thess. 2:9 (ESV), 1 Tim. 4:1 (ESV), Prov. 7:1-27 (ESV)

end, you will finally realize "For her house leads down to death and her paths to the spirits of the dead". "They will throw them into the fiery furnace, where there will be weeping and gnashing of teeth. That house belongs to a prophetess who teaches and seduces many to practice sexual immorality.[51]

I am the unchaste spirit of Jezebel; I am the spirit of seduction, lust and perversion. I specifically promote confusions of God's gift of romance and love. I work together with the spirit of religion to sabotage all the preferences of the Lord God. I make it all seem right to a man; I want these fools to see the benefits, it will all seem right to them, but in the end it will lead to death. Yes, hear me you foolish men, I Jezebel will prostitute you into becoming treacherous, reckless, swollen with conceit, lovers of pleasure rather than lovers of God". I know you well, and what does the scripture say about you, "Which of the prophets did your fathers not persecute? And they killed those who announced beforehand the coming of the Righteous One, whom you have now betrayed and murdered". You belong to me.[52]

---

51   Prov. 9:18 (NIV), Prov. 5:5 (NIV), Rev. 22:15 (NIV), Prov. 2:18 (NIV), Matt. 13:42 (NIV), Rev. 2:20 (ISV)

52   Enlow (2008), Prov. 14:12 (KJV), Rom. 6:21 (NIV), Prov. 12:15 (NIV), 2 Tim. 3:4 (NIV), Acts 7:52 (ESV)

The Thoughts of Essay 11

The enemy discusses his feelings on seduction. What are your beliefs on seducing spirits?

Consider the following scriptures:

The Spirit clearly says that in later times some will abandon the faith and follow deceiving spirits and things taught by demons, 1 Timothy 4:1.

Who are you following?

How long will this continue in the hearts of these lying prophets, who prophesy the delusions of their own minds? Jeremiah 23:26.

Can you identify lying (false prophets)?

The Philistine rulers came to her and said, "Trick him, and find out what makes him so strong. Find out how we can overpower him. We want to tie him up in order to torture him. Each of us will give you 1,100 pieces of silver." Judges 16:5.

Can you identify the enemy's schemes and tricks?

So Delilah said to Samson, "Tell me the secret of your great strength and how you can be tied up and subdued." Judges 16:6.

The enemy is always plotting against you, he has no mercy, and you have no strength to fight him on your own, your great strength is the WORD, it is the LORD JESUS. "Draw your sword and strike a blow, run the enemy through, right to the bone and marrow of this demon spirit."

They commit adultery with their eyes, and their desire for sin is never satisfied. They lure unstable people into sin, and they are well trained in greed. They live under God's curse. 2 Peter 2:14

How unstable are you?

He is a double-minded man, unstable in all he does. James 1:8.

Be of sound mind and body, resist and fight back with the power of the Lord. Learn & memorize 2 Timothy 3:16. Review the scriptures of essay 11, review the references.

Essay 12: Fear and Terror

I want to control your existence; I want your life to be in doubt day and night. I want you to live in fear; I want you to have no guarantee of living a long, happy and peaceful life. I want you to live under the influence of terror and worry. When there is love, fear cannot exist. I hate love and I do not want you to feel love, I do not want you to be loved. I have false prophets and teachers among you; they will introduce destructive heresies and lies that will deny the truth about the Lord's plan of salvation thus bringing swift destruction upon you.[53]

I want your money, I love money, I want you to love money, I want to influence you to store up for yourselves treasures on earth. Do anything and everything you can to increase your riches and set your heart on them. I want you to steal and conceal the things you have taken. I want you to rob from your father and your mother. I want you to steal from the widows and the fatherless, take what is not yours, and most importantly, steal from God.[54]

I want you to live like people of the world; I want you to be controlled by your old sinful nature, your spirit must be smothered and you must be dead in Christ; I do not want you to be delivered from my bondage and you must avoid the Spirit of Truth, I do not want you to know the truth, you must not be free from me. You must quench the Spirit when it speaks to you. As I have said many times, I am deception; I have underground influences that will bring about chaos. I was able to deceive 1/3 of the

---

53 Deut. 28:66 (ESV), Bonnke (1996), 1 John 4:18 (NIV), 2 Pet. 2:1 (NIV)
54 1 Tim. 6:10 (ESV), Matt. 6:19 (NIV), Joshua 7:21 (NIV), Psalm 62:10 (NIV), Prov. 28:24 (NIV), Prov. 19:26 (NIV), Isa. 10:2 (NIV), Titus 2:10 (DBY), Mal. 3:8-9 (NIV)

angels in heaven, I was able to deceive Eve in the garden, I have clandestine plans to deceive the whole world.[55]

I am the master of the natural and the fleshly, I want control of your mind, you must walk in the flesh, and I will have impact on your will, destroy your body, damage your emotions and keep your spirit dead to God. You see I want to create havoc in the lives of God's creation, even the entire planet. I want all of you afflicted with diseases, poverty, strife, misery and confusion. The whole world, all of creation groans because of me, I will turn this planet into a wasteland by manipulating the wicked and yes, all of the animals and birds will perish. I am your worst nightmare, many of you do not know I exist; many of you refuse to believe that I exist and as for those of you who do believe I exist, I have many tricks planned for you as well. We have no power over Jesus, but we have power over you unbelieving fools, those of you who are condemned. If you have not accepted the Holy One, you are mine.

---

55 1 Cor. 3:3 (NIV), Anderson (2000), Rom. 8:1-25 (NASB), John 14:17 (NIV), John 8:32 (ISV), 1 Thess. 5:19 (NIV), Bevere (2001), Rev. 12:9 (ESV)

The Thoughts of Your Enemy in Essay 12 Wants You to Live in Fear and Terror

WHAT ARE YOUR VIEWS? SELAH

Think about the following-what does the scripture say?

(1). the thief's purpose is to steal and kill and destroy. My purpose is to give them a rich and satisfying life. John 10:10.

Is it not obvious that the enemy is a thief? He uses fear and terror to steal your life from you. Observe what is going on; look at yourself, observe your mate, watch your family, consider what is happening in our society, gaze upon your community, behold our nation and our world. All that we see, hear and talk about is fear and terror. Death stalks us, day and night, looking for the opportunity to strike.

(2). yet you refuse to come to me to have life. John 5:40.

Is it not obvious that Jesus is the answer to fear and terror? But the world refuses Him. He is despised and rejected by those already marked for destruction. Snubbed and turned down, mankind says no to Jesus. Isaiah 53:3. Mankind would rather live in fear and terror, believing under the enemy's deception that they can defeat fear and terror without the saving power of the ONE who conquered death.

Listen to this:
"For there is one God, and one mediator between God and men, the man Christ Jesus;" 1 Timothy 2:5.

Review the scriptures in the footnotes of essay 12 and the references. Many will go to their grave having died under the influence of deception and not LIFE.

Essay 13: I can make you do whatever I want

I am the master of disobedience and I have many ways to trick you and cause you to disobey God, I want you to use your human reasoning to justify your disobedience. I want to see you apply your rational thinking. I can blind you with deception and make you believe that partial obedience is just as good as full obedience. You are too stupid to understand that there are consequences for disobedience. Look at what happen to Adam and Eve, Cain, Ananias and Sapphira, and let's not forget King Saul. These are but a few of the souls I have tricked into disobedience. I will mislead you away from the ways of God by influencing you to follow the path of rebellion. The fun part of all this insubordination is that most of the times you won't even know you are being deceived.[56]

I am the Lord of Rebellion; it is my goal to influence you to disobey the word of the Lord. Rebel and give me access to your mind, allow me to cover your eyes and lead you to areas that will permit me to use my power to attack you. I desire to control you; I will have my way with you. The unbeliever is mine, they will join me in the lake of fire, the believer belongs to the Lord, but I can control them when they rebel against Gods word, they will open themselves up to witchcraft through their disobedience and I will afflict them with all that I have.[57]

I am the spirit of anti-Christ. I am that spirit that denies that Jesus Christ is come in the flesh, and I deny that He is from God. I will show you a way that seems right when it comes to practicing worship. It is called religion,

---

56 (Bevere, 2001, Chapter 5), Gen. 4:4-5 (NLT), Acts 5:1-11 (ESV), 1 Sam. 13:13 (ESV)

57 1 Sam. 15:23 (NLT), (Bevere, 2001, Chapter 6), Rev. 20:15 (ISV), Rev. 20:10 (NIV), Ps. 13:2 (NIV), Ps. 39:11 (NIV)

the traditions of men. I want you to set aside the commandments of God and follow your traditions; I will guide you in the many ways of learning and following the traditions of the world. I will encourage you to use human wisdom; the message of the cross is foolishness.[58]

I will show you wisdom; you will learn knowledge through philosophy and scientific reasoning, you will gain insight into the ability to discern the inner qualities of human relationships, I will show you how to develop good sense, you will be taught the accepted beliefs of the ancients, you will know how to think and take action with your own human strength, you must turn away from the foolishness and weakness of God and learn of man's wisdom and strength. Do not accept the things that come from the Spirit of God. It is all foolishness. You must live by human reasoning, you must have vision and be sensitive to your surroundings, and these are the kind of things that will put you on the path of enlightenment. You must have the wisdom of this world, and I will give the world to you.[59]

My demons have plans to control your mind through deceptions.

---

58 1 John 2:22 (NIV), James 1:27 (NLT), Prov. 14:12 (ASV), Mark 7:8 (NASB), Col. 2:8 (KJB), 1 Cor. 1:21 (NLT), 1 Cor. 1:18 (NIV)
59 (Merriam-Webster's, 2011, wisdom), 1 Cor. 1:25 (NIV), 1 Cor. 2:14 (NIV), (Bevere, 2001, Chapter 7), Matt. 4:8-9 (ESV)

The Thoughts of the enemy in Essay 13 Concerning His Desires to Manipulate the Human Race

WHAT ARE YOUR THEORIES ON THE ENEMYS MOTIVES? SELAH

The enemy knows he can make the unbelievers do whatever he wants them to do. 2 Corinthian 4:4 tell us that, "The god of this age has blinded the minds of unbelievers, so that they cannot see the light of the gospel of the glory of Christ, who is the image of God."

We also know that the enemy can make believers do whatever he wants them to do. 2 Corinthians 2:11 tell us; "Lest Satan should get an advantage of us: for we are not ignorant of his devices". The believer in Christ can be outwitted, outsmarted, taken advantage of, and overreached.

We know that the enemy can seduce nations. Nahum 3:4 tells us that "Because of the multitude of the prostitutions of the well favored harlot, the mistress of witchcrafts, that sells nations through her prostitutions and families through her witchcrafts".

"We must battle this principality that dominates our nation".

The unbeliever can be manipulated by satanic forces, they have no power to fight these evil personalities because they have no authority through Jesus to resist and make them flee. The believer has the authority to battle these demonic forces but very often they are helpless because of sin or lack of faith. The major difference between the two is that the unbeliever is on their way to hell. The believer who is saved and on their way to heaven can live a defeated life and be of little use to the kingdom.

Review the scriptures of the footnotes in essay 13, review the references. Think on them.

Essay 14: The Family Tree

I want the family; I want control of the human family, I want to take a respectable family tree and turn it into a wicked family tree. Adam and Eve were my first family, they fell for my deception. They were my first rebellious couple; I showed them how to desire and gain worldly wisdom, I showed them how they can become gods by having the knowledge of good and evil. I was working on a plan to further their insubordination by having them partake of the tree of life, but the Lord threw them out of the garden and placed cherubim to guard its entrance and to protect the tree of life. They came close to living forever in disobedience and rebellion but my plan was ruin. I shall never give up; I will keep trying new tricks and develop new plans to continue my evil deceptions.[60]

I want your seed, I want to teach them disobedience, rebellion, anger, jealousy, hate and murder, Cain was Adam and Eves first born and he was the world's first murder, he was an angry man, he was the kind of man I could disciple. Through him I was able to gain control over his family tree and expand my influence of sin. Through my wanderings about the earth I have promoted evil, wickedness, corruption, immorality, depravity and debauchery. I am ruthless, merciless, cruel and shameless. I love to steal, kill and destroy. What is yours is mind, and what you hope to get belongs to me. The human family tree is under my control. If you do not have Jesus in your life, you can do nothing to stop me; I will sift you like wheat. I will bring plagues and accidents and all sorts of tragic circumstances into your family tree. Why am I doing all of these things to you? The answer is easy. I hate you. I hate you because God loves you, and I hate God, you

---

60   Matt. 7:18 (ISV), Gen. 3:6 (NIV), Gen. 3:22-24 (NASB)

see unlike you I believe in God, and I fear Him, He makes me tremble but you don't fear God, do you? [61]

I have planted the seeds of corruption on the earth, the trees of dishonesty and depravity will grow strong and mighty, and they will bear much fruit; dishonesty will bring forth the fruit of exploitation, sleaze, bribery, fraud, venality and vice. Depravity will bring forth the fruit of perversion, immorality, harm, debasement and degeneracy. When these fruits fall to the ground and begin to decay, they will germinate into the seeds of disobedience, human reasoning, pride, insubordination, rebellion and evil communication. I will snatch up off the ground any good seed before it gives birth to righteousness, justice and recompense. You do not have understanding, you lack knowledge, I have blinded you so that you cannot see, and I have closed your ears so that you cannot hear. God is using the simple message of the gospel to save you, but you refuse Him. Therefore, you; your family and you're possessions belong to me and we will spend eternity together in an unbearable environment of torment, suffering and terror, forever separated from the God who sent you an invitation, that you refused. [62]

---

61 (Bevere , 2001, chapter 15), Gen. 4:9-15 (NASB), Prov. 29:22 (NLT), Gen. 4:16-24 (NASB), Luke 22:31 (KJV), Job 2:1-10, John 3:16, James 2:19 (ISV)
62 Matt. 15:19 (NIV), Rom. 1:28 (NIV), Psalm 14:1 (NIV), Prov. 6:18 (NIV), Matt. 13:1-9 (NIV), Heb. 10:31 (NASB), Prov. 21:21 (NIV), Matt. 22:1-14 (ESV), Rev. 20:11-15 (ESV)

The Thoughts of the Enemy Concerning Essay 14

The enemy wants our family and he wants to establish a revolution in the household. He wants to encourage mutiny, agitation, insurrection, an uprising, a revolt. He wants to create a new family unit, one that will be classified in a different category that promotes an alternate life style. Free from the traditional family established by God.

What do we know about rebellion?

"But there were also false prophets among the people, just as there will be false teachers among you. They will secretly introduce destructive heresies, even denying the sovereign Lord who bought them--bringing swift destruction on themselves". 2 Peter 2:1.

"If you keep on biting and devouring each other, watch out or you will be destroyed by each other". Galatians 5:15.

"No doubt there have to be differences among you to show which of you have God's approval". 1 Corinthians 11:19.

"For I am afraid that when I come I may not find you as I want you to be, and you may not find me as you want me to be. I fear that there may be quarreling, jealousy, outbursts of anger, factions, slander, gossip, arrogance and disorder". 2 Corinthians 12:20.

"Idolatry, drug use, hatred, rivalry, jealousy, angry outbursts, selfish ambition, conflict, factions". Galatians 5:20.

This is not a Christian family; it is today's nuclear family.

Review the scriptures and references of essay 14.

Essay 15: I am Sovereign

I am the Black robed master, ruler of the planet earth, all human political and judicial power is under my influence and control, I have power and rule over all the highest human authorities, I have sway and domination of persons who have the power to make decisions, I manipulate and command all agencies whose judgments or opinions are considered to be authoritative. I am the arbiter; I am the principality that has power over judges to judge others. I hold this position because I stole your God given authority from you. God gave it to you and you gave it to me through your ignorance and lack of resistance. I have no intentions of giving it back to you and there is nothing you can do to make me.[63]

I am the great deceiver; I will provide revelation to the elite and they will rule the ignorant. I will provide guidance into all areas of the knowledge of good and evil. I am responsible for misleading the uninformed. I am the sovereign head of the nations who oversees the darkness that influences flesh and blood. It is me the cosmic power who controls spiritual wickedness in high places, you know who I am, but you are too smart to believe in my existence. Because of your unbelief, you will not see the flaming darts I will be firing at you, you will die, and I will have access to your spirit and you will scream in horror as you see and feel the eternal damnation that awaits you.[64]

I am the tyrant, the spirit of cruelty, lord of the unjust, ruler of the law, hater of fairness and I will tyrannize all the people of the earth, I oppose

---

63 (Merriam-Webster, 2011, sovereign), Gen. 1: 28 (ESV), Matt. 7:1-6 (NASB), (Sutherland, 2005, Chapter 2 & 12), Dan. 2: 44 (ESV), Dan. 7: 18, 27 (ESV)
64 Hosea 4:6 (ESV), Prov. 29:18 (GWT), (Sutherland, 2005, Chapter 3), Eph. 6: 12 (AKJV)

Bob Jackson

the gospel of Christ, and I dispute the word of God. Your laws will be my laws and my laws will be what I say it will be. I will place my thoughts in you and your thoughts will be my thoughts and you will do what I tell you. All mankind will live in this world by the rules of the commander of the power in the unseen world. You are a fool and no fool can stop me.[65]

I will have my demons gather small groups of corrupt and selfish humans to exercise control over you through your governments and you shall do my bidding. I will get rid of your Godly laws and place you under my absolute power and authority, I will be the unseen strongman, through your unbelief of my existence and your denial of He who God has sent to save you, I will destroy you and all of those like you. Hell was created for me and my angels, but by your rebellion against God, you will join me there in everlasting torment. I will be your eternal choir master; you shall scream the songs of pain and horror continuously and forever, amen.[66]

---

65 Acts 19:9 (ESV), Ask.com (2011), John 3:16 (ESV), 2 Tim. 3:16 (ESV), Hab. 1:4 (ESV), Ps. 119:126 (NIV), Rom. 1:21 (NIV), 2 Thess. 2:11 (NIV), Ex. 20:3 (ESV), (Sutherland, 2005, Chapter 7), Eph. 2:2 (NLT), Isa. 55:8 (ASV), Ps. 53:1 (ESV)
66 (Southerland, 2005, Chapter 10), (Merriam-Webster, 2011, oligarchy), Matt. 25:41 (ESV)

The Thoughts of Essay 15

Your Enemy's dynamic assertions

Review the scriptures and references in the footnotes for essay 15. Try to understand the thoughts of the enemy. Ask yourself these questions? How is he able to deceive the ruling powers of our society? How is he able to mislead them? How is he able to trick and gain control of our rulers?

The following scriptures talk about deception:

"Timothy, guard what has been entrusted to your care. Turn away from godless chatter and the opposing ideas of what is falsely called knowledge". 1 Tim. 6:20.

Our judicial system is considered to be full of knowledge and yet they generally oppose Godly ideas, Christian values and seem to promote humanistic principles. Our judicial system opposes the display of the Ten Commandments in public areas while it is displayed in the Supreme Court. It is hard at work creating laws to support its views and is trying to re-write the US Constitution, a law that has been entrusted to our care.

"See to it that no one takes you captive by philosophy and empty deceit, according to human tradition, according to the elemental spirits of the world, and not according to Christ". Colossians 2:8.

It would appear that our judicial system has established its own philosophy according to human tradition and the spirits of this world. They lack knowledge and understanding. They are changing our government and society with empty deceptions. Their rule of law is to change our values, beliefs, thinking and our way of life.

What have you noticed about our judicial system?

Essay 16: I have the key to your mind

I know you very well. I have been studying you, I know what you want, I know what you desire, and I will use that knowledge to destroy you. I will put my thoughts in you and watch your body, mind and spirit fall apart. I will use thought control to cause you to become obese, I will use my powers of suggestion to cause you to desire strong drink, I will encourage you to use your reasoning to justify the use of tobacco, drugs and sweets. All that you see and hear, you shall lust after it, you shall desire it and it will consume you and bring devastation to your fleshly body. [67]

I know you very well. You are born with a rebellious spirit. It is so easy for me to take advantage of you. I will have my way with you. I will work day and night to encourage you to eat the things that are unhealthy for you, I will encourage you to drink the things that are unhealthy for you, I will encourage you to become physically lazy, I will introduce various diseases into your body, and I will make you weak and sick. I have declared war against the Lords anointed, I will lay siege on the carnal mind, I will thoroughly confuse the double minded, I will constantly attack your defenses and communications, and I will put you through the fires of life. [68]

I know you very well. You are stubborn, you will not listen, and you are selfish. You reject the truth but believe the lie. I am the father of lies and I can tell you anything I want, and you will believe. I have perverted your thinking. "Does not the scripture say that God will send you strong

---

67 (Meyer, 1995, Chapter 1), Prov. 20:1 (NIV), Prov. 23:20-21, 30 (NIV), Isa. 5:11 (NLT), 1 Cor. 8:8 (NIV), I Cor. 3:17 (NIV)

68 (Meyer, 1995, Chapters 2, 3 & 7), Prov. 17:11 (ESV), Rev. 13:7 (NASB), James 1:8 (ISV), 2 Peter 2:14 (KJB), James 3:6 (NLT), Job 2:1-7 (NIV)

delusions that you shall believe the lie"? You are such a fool, if you keep rejecting the truth, you will believe the lie. You lack understanding, you lack wisdom, and you will not hear the Lords warnings. When you refuse to hear Him, you end up hearing me. You are just like me, "Condemned already".[69]

I know you very well. You have fear, dread, anxiety, horror, distress, fright, panic, worry and concerns. I am your worst nightmare and you don't even know it. I control you, I own you and I can turn you in whatever direction I want you to go, you are my slave. I am the unseen secret power in your life. You have no control over your thoughts. Your mind is full of trash and junk; your communication is wicked, obnoxious, nasty and foul. You will not enter Gods kingdom because you are my disciple. All of my disciples do not have their name listed in the Lambs book of life. You will die and spend eternity with me in the abyss. [70]

69 Gal. 5:20 (NIV), 2 Kings 17:40 (AJKV), Jer. 5:23 (GWT), Jer. 6:17 (ASV), Jer. 7:28 (ESV), John 8:44 (NIV), 2 Thess. 2:11 (NIV), John 14:6 (NIV), Prov. 8:1 (NIV), John 16:11 (NLT)
70 Rom. 12:2 (NIV), Col. 3:10 (NIV), Eph. 4:23 (NLT), Eph. 4:29 (ISV), Eph. 5:4 (NIV), Rev. 20:15 (NIV)

The Thoughts on Essay 16

Your Enemy's thoughts towards forceful declarations

Review the scriptures and references in the footnotes for essay 16. Try to understand the thoughts of the enemy. Ask yourself these questions? How is he able to influence us? How is he able to manipulate and gain power over us?

The enemy has perverted the minds of mankind. The enemy has a strategy for perversion; he has a plan to pollute the mind. Examine your environment? What do you see? What are you hearing? What is being communicated? What is the cause of reprobation?

Read Hosea Chapter4 & 5, Study Romans chapter 1, Look at (Phillips, 2010, chapter 20). We live in a perverted society. Our society is corrupt, depraved, warped and degenerate. The enemy has twisted the minds of men and women. All that we see, hear and speak has become abnormal. Our society does not know the difference between truth and error, it no longer knows the variance between rights and wrong, it cannot separate good from evil. Mankind is spiritually separated from the knowledge of God and is doomed.

We are being led astray by the demons of perversion

Essay 17: Religion is the way to reach God

I am the false teacher, I will show you the way to God. I will show you how to get to God. The way I will point out to you is filled with tradition, the tradition of men, it is the way to the true God; it is the way to eternal life, it is the way to communicate with God. I have placed in your path an alternate way to worship. I have assigned a host of deceiving spirits with the doctrine of demons, legions of hypocritical liars who will corrupt your minds. They are full of godless myths and old wives tails. They will lead you to the way which will seem right to you. You are not wise, you are a fool, and I will guide you. I have wise men. I have scholars. I have philosophers of this age. I will guide you into the wisdom of this world. [71]

You must work your way to eternal life. You will use my plan, I will show you how to lay the foundation, I will show you how to lay the corner stone, and I will show you how to build a tower to God. I will teach you how to use your religion to work your way to heaven. Does not the scripture say "faith without works is dead?" The earth is once again communicating in one language. I will show you how to use your human mind to understand the many ways of worshiping. Is there really only one way to get to God? You must use your rational thinking in order to know and understand the sensibleness of the truth.[72]

I have introduced a true means of worship into the minds of men. The kind of worship that is suitable to all mankind. It is designed to appeal to every ethnic group. They are the religions from the four corners of the

---

71   John 14:6 (NIV), 1 John 5:20 (NIV), Matt 15:6 (ASV), 1 Tim. 4:1-16 (NIV), Prov. 16:25 (NIV), Prov. 12:15 (NIV), 1 Cor. 1:20 (NIV)
72   James 2:17 (ESV), Eph. 2:8-9 (ESV), Gen. 11:4 (ESV), Eph. 5:6-12 (AKJV), 1 John 4:1 (AKJV), John 14:6 (AKJV), (Meyer, 1995, Chapter 10)

earth. You can worship your god, gods or no god. These religions are controlled by familiar spirits, wizards, sorcerers, fornicators, murderers, idolaters, and liars. These are the abominable. They are my demons; they will be your spirit guide. They will lead you to enlightenment and when your time on earth is complete, they will lead you into your world of the second death.[73]

73 Lev. 19:31 (AKJV), James 4:7 (AKJV), Rev. 22:15 (AKJV), Eph. 6:12 (AKJV), Rev. 21:8 (AKJV)

The Thoughts of Essay 17

Your Enemy's thoughts are powerful, think on them, Selah

What is a false teacher?

"These false teachers are like unthinking animals, creatures of instinct, born to be caught and destroyed. They scoff at things they do not understand, and like animals, they will be destroyed". 2 Peter 2:12.

Can you work your way to eternal life?

No, the scripture says, "For by grace you have been saved through faith. And this is not your own doing; it is the gift of God; not as a result of works, so that no one may boast". Ephesians 2:8-9.

What is a true means of worship?

"But you shall serve the LORD your God, and He will bless your bread and your water; and I will remove sickness from your midst". Exodus 23:25.

Review the scriptures and references. Study them. Think of them.

Wake up; "Your enemy's way is not Gods way".

Essay 18: Confusion

I am confusion, I will pour together a new thing, and I will commingle and cause trouble to the institution of marriage. I will stir up doubts and unbelief's about marriage between a man and a woman. This new thing I will introduce into the minds of the human race, it is an old thing that will be re-established as marriage between members of the same sex. I will stir up the unnatural desires in the minds of the natural man and they shall change their laws and pervert the sacred institution that God has created. Homosexual activity and marriages shall be legal. I will wage war on your society and make you except the homosexual agenda, and they will do detestable things.[74]

I will take control of your mind. There will be no more of this being fruitful and multiply, there can be no more populating of the earth. Two males cannot be fruitful and increase the population. Two females cannot be fruitful and increase the population. Gay civil unions and gay marriages cannot produce a living soul. They will use each other up until the day they die. I will use this new thing to depopulate the nations, communities will cease to exist and nation building will be destroyed. Your leadership will be corrupted and pass away. You will no longer fill the earth and subdue it. You will no longer rule over the fish of the sea and the birds of the air; you will no longer rule over every living creature that moves on the ground. I will educate the minds of the young through entertainment. This new thing will be communicated all over the earth. I shall attack the family by redefining it to include the homosexual itinerary, "my plan". Young children shall have two fathers and two mothers. God's establishment of

---

74 Vines Expository, Jude 1:7-8 (ESV), 2 Peter 2:2 (NIV), Lev. 18:22 (NLT), Rom. 1:27 (NIV), Lev. 20:13 (NIV), (Sears & Olsten, 2003, Chapter 1)

one man and one woman will no longer exist. I will control the minds of God's creation.[75]

I have said in my heart, I will ascend into heaven, I will exalt my throne above the stars of God; and I will sit upon the mount of congregation, in the uttermost parts of the north. I am a god, "I am god; I sit on the throne of a god in the heart of the seas." I will oppose and will exalt myself over everything that is called God or is worshiped, so that I will sit in God's temple, proclaiming myself to be God. There is no human who can bring me down to the ground. [76]

I am Leviathan. You cannot catch me with your hooks; nothing on earth is equal to me, I am a creature without fear. I am a reptile with sharp teeth. I will rip you to pieces. I will tear you apart. You will be consumed. I am the fleeing serpent, I am the twisted serpent, as you move about in this world, I am with you, and I am the hidden King over all the children of pride.[77]

---

75   Gen. 9:7 (NASB), Gen. 35:11 (NIV), Gen. 1:28 (NIV), Gen. 9:1 (NIV), (Sears & Olsten, 2003, Chapter 2, 5 &6)

76   Isa. 14:13 (ASV), Ezek. 28:2 (NIV), 2 Thess. 2:4 (NIV), Obad. 1:3 (NIV), Luke 10:18 (ISV), Rev. 12:9 (NIV)

77   Job 41:1-6, (NIV), Job 41:30-34 (NIV), Bible Encyclopedia-Leviathan, (Phillips, 2010, Chapter 21), Ps 104:26 (NASB), Isa 27:1 (NIV)

The Thoughts of Essay 18

Your Enemy's thoughts are haunting, think about it, Selah

Who is this monster?

Does this sound familiar? "His tail swept a third of the stars out of the sky and flung them to the earth. The dragon stood in front of the woman who was about to give birth, so that he might devour her child the moment it was born". Revelation 12:4.

What is pride?

"Pride leads to conflict; those who take advice are wise". Proverbs 13:10.

"Pride goes before destruction, a haughty spirit before a fall". Proverbs 16:18.

"When pride comes, then come disgrace, but with the humble is wisdom". Proverbs 11:2.

"A man's pride shall bring him low: but honor shall uphold the humble in spirit". Proverbs 29:23.

"The fear of the LORD is to hate evil; Pride and arrogance and the evil way and the perverted mouth, I hate". Proverbs 8:13.

Review the scriptures and the references. Think about the confusion that exists in this world.

So then, "Where does pride come from"?

Essay 19: A Powerful Delusion

I will send to the world a powerful delusion, I will cause split-personalities to be developed in the minds of men, I will use my influence to gain control of the world. I will take advantage of man's ignorance about my existence and manipulation and I will set about destroying the entire human race, even the very elect if it can be possible. I will pass upon them a persistently psychotic belief, a big lie and they will receive it. [78]

Man is foolish, if he hears the truth, he will not believe the truth, if he hears a lie; that he will believe. Humans are easy to deceive; they will listen to my demonic suggestions. They will believe my clairvoyants, they will listen to my spiritualists, they will heed to my commentators of dreams, they will pay attention to my agents and wizards and they will believe my lies, and they will obey, they will serve me as god and will deny the true God. They will all become my disciples and turn their souls over to me by default. Humans think they are too smart to believe in God and they do not believe that I exist, mankind wants no part of God, and they hate God, and will try to avoid Him. They do not realize that I hate both God and Man. Man is just like me, he is cursed and he will go to where I am going when time comes to an end.[79]

I will torment humans all of their days on earth. I will charge my demons to make them suffer; I will bring terror upon them, I will bring horror and anguish upon them, there will be great distress all over the earth. Humans will suffer, the animals will suffer, the fish and creeping things,

---

78 2 Thess.2:11 (NIV), Merriam-Webster's-Delusions, (Shoebat and Richardson, 2010, Chapter 16), Rom. 1:28 (NIV), 2 Thess. 2:11 (KJB), 2 Tim. 4:4 (NIV), James 1:8 (NIV), Psalm 92:6 (NIV), 1 John 4:1 (NIV), Matt. 24:24 (ESV)

79 Matt. 24:4 (NIV), Jer. 27:9 (NIV), Matt.25:41 (NIV), 1 John 4:20 (NIV), (Wiese, 2008, Chapter 9), Matt. 8:29 (NIV), Lev. 19:31 (NIV)

birds and plants will suffer. All of man's environment will be under great distress. I will spare no one and nothing. I will even attack the innocent. The earth is mine; God took it from me and gave it to you. And because of your disobedience and ignorance you forfeited it back to me. I will not give it back to you without a fight. I will maintain control of this world in the same manner I have always held control, by secretly using the power of suggestion, manipulation and deception.[80]

I am the man of sin, I am the adversary, I am the "Shinning One Son of the Morning Star", I am the "Shining Brilliant One", I am the "Crescent Moon", I am a god, and you will worship me, you shall bow before me and pray to me, I shall guide you until your end comes and then you shall get your reward, eternal terror in the abyss.[81]

80 Job 15:20 (NLT), Job 15:24 (NIV), Job 27:13 (NIV), Jer. 9:6 (NASB), Det. 8:10 (NIV)
81 Isa. 14:12-14 (NIV), Rev. 9:1 (NIV), Rev. 9:11 (NIV), John 8:44 (NIV), (Shoebat and Richardson, 2010, Chapter 82), 2 Thess. 2:3 (ISV)

The Thoughts of Essay 19

Your Enemy's thoughts are unforgettable, think about it, Selah

What is this strong delusion?

The enemy wants to establish a disordered state of mind. He wants you to fall prey to the synonyms of delusion, such things as error, falsehood, old wives' tales, untruth, hallucination, illusions and misbelief, etc.[82]

The enemy lies, listen to the scripture:

"And for this cause God shall send them strong delusion, that they should believe a lie". 2 Thessalonians 2:11.

"You belong to your father the devil, and you want to carry out the desires of your father. He was a murderer from the beginning and has never stood for truth, since there is no truth in him. Whenever he tells a lie he speaks in character, because he is a liar and the father of lies". John 8:44.

The enemy thinks of you as a fool

The enemy knows that there is a God, he believes in God and tremble, but man is a fool because he believes that there is no God, and in sheer stupidity excepts death in his sinful condition.

Man is corrupt, he is an abomination:

"To the choirmaster. Of David. The fool says in his heart, "There is no God." They are corrupt, they do abominable deeds, there is none who does good". Psalm 14:1.

"You believe that there is one God. That's fine! Even the demons believe that and tremble with fear". James 2:19.

82　See references "Merriam-Webster" delusion

"[One day] the evil spirit answered them, "Jesus I know, and I know about Paul, but who are you?". Acts 19:15.

Review the scriptures and references in the footnotes for essay 19. Try to understand the thoughts of the enemy. Ask yourself these questions? How does the enemy expose us to delusions? How is he able to manipulate the mind?

Essay 20: The god of this world

I am the god of this age; I am the one who blinds the minds of the unbelievers, I am the one who makes it possible that you cannot see the light of the gospel of the glory of Christ, the true one who is the image of God. Your eyes will remain shut; you shall see nothing but darkness, you shall not see the light. I have power, I am Satan, and I will keep you away from God. You will die in your sins; I will keep you from finding your place of sanctification through faith in God.[83]

No human can outwit me, and no unbelieving sinner can outsmart me, none of you are aware of my schemes. You have no self-control, you are not alert, I will catch you, I will gain access to your mind, I will enslave you, and I will devour you. I will slay all those who refuse to worship me. I am not your savior, I am not your redeemer, I am god, and you will bend the knee and worship me, I will be exalted. There is no god but me. All those who follow me will be morally corrupted, and all who refuse me will be destroyed. I will reach high into the sky. I will soar like an eagle and watch for prey. Some I will harass (The redeemed), and others I will consume (The condemned). I will have no mercy on the condemened.[84]

I am the great monster who controls the nations; we will war against the Lords anointed. I will be a thorn to them who refuse to follow me. I am perfection, I am beautiful, I have wisdom, and I the young lion will lead the nations who worship me. All those who choose to reject Father Gods appointed Way to Him-self by design or default belong to me and they will

---

83 2 Cor. 4:4-5 (ESV), (Shoebat & Richardson, 2010, Chapter 12), 2 Cor. 4:4 (NIV), Acts 28:16 (NIV), 2 Cor. 2:11 (NIV)

84 2 Cor. 2:11 (GWT), 1 Pet. 5:8 (NIV), (Shoebat & Richardson, 2010, Chapter 12 & 13), Judg. 19:22-30 (ESV), Obad. 1:4 (NIV), John 3:18 (NIV), Prov. 2:14 (NIV)

obey me. I have an appointed way of worship that you must follow, it is my counterfeit religion, it is how you are to worship me, there are rules, there are regulations, there is harsh treatment of the flesh, and there is humility, but there is no love, only obedience. [85]

I am the true prince of peace. I will show you the path of justice and lead you to reconciliation; I will put you onto the road of goodwill. As the god of this world you shall know peace as I see it. You shall know peace as I decree it. When you growl and moan, I shall show you how to earn your deliverance. You shall have rest. Look toward me, I am the light, gaze upon me and see my brightness. I have a much better message to preach to you, a message that you can understand, a message that you will appreciate. I am the angel of light and I have good news, news that comes from the heavenly realm. If you will fall down and worship me I will give you the world and all of its glory.[86]

---

85 Ezek. 29:3 (NIV), (Shoebat & Richardson, 2010, Chapter 58), Ezek. 28:12 (NIV), Ezek. 32:2 (NIV), Hos. 5:7 (NIV), Isa. 1:14 (NIV), Isa. 48:8 (NIV), Col. 2:23 (ESV), Col. 2:8 (NIV), Col. 2:18 (NIV), 1 Tim. 4:3 (NIV)

86 Isa. 59:8 (NIV), (Shoebat & Richardson, 2010, Chapter 30), Isa. 57:21 (NIV), Isa. 59 :9 & 11 (NIV), Isa. 57 :20 (NIV), 2 Cor. 11 :14 (ESV), Gal. 1 :8 (NIV), Matt. 4 :8-9(NIV)

The Thoughts on Essay 20

The opinions of your enemy - The god of this world

Review the scriptures and references listed for each paragraph in the footnotes for essay 20. Study them, think on them, speak them out loud, and meditate on them.

Who is the god of this world and what does he do?

"Satan, who is the god of this world, has blinded the minds of those who don't believe. They are unable to see the glorious light of the Good News. They don't understand this message about the glory of Christ, who is the exact likeness of God". 2 Corinthians 4:4.

What are Gods intentions?

"To open their eyes and turn them from darkness to light and from the power of Satan to God, so that they may receive forgiveness of sins and a place among those who are sanctified by faith in me". Acts 26:18.

What did God give to us?

"Who gave himself for our sins to rescue us from the present evil age, according to the will of our God and Father". Galatians 1:4.

What are your thoughts?

Essay 21: The Ruler of Foul Spirits

I am the lord of foul spirits. I take possession of the minds and bodies of humans, and eventually I will take their souls as well. I have many unclean spirits who have the power to cause harm to the body and the mind. They will shut your mouth, keep you from speaking, and make you deaf so that you cannot hear, quiet your spirit and make it dead. Yes it is me Satan, the power of darkness, I want your body, and a body especially made for the fires of hell. There is excitement in the place of the dead, many of your family and friends will be there, they may know that you are in the pit, but they won't know what part you are in. There is too much turmoil going on, lots of pain, yelling and screaming. Because of your unbelief the Lord will send you to the pit, it is full of souls like you, I have a place for you and my demons will give you their full attention, they will have no mercy. My demons will shout profanity as they torture you for eternity and you cannot sing praises to the Lord because you have gone into the silence of the grave.[87]

I am the Lord of Sheol. I would like to have you whole; I want you to come down to the pit alive, but dead or alive it does not matter, your destiny is to enter to the center of the earth where there is a lake of fire, it is a deep underground chamber, it is hotter than hot, where fire and sulfur runs like a river, it is always in motion, it is never full of souls, there is plenty of room, does not the scripture say, that "death and hell are never satisfied". I look forward to accusing you humans, "God's creation". You are busy doing my bidding, you are removing the name of the true God from your society, and you are busy removing all memory of the Holy One from your history. All memorials, writing, monuments will be struck down from

---

87 Mark 9:25 (NLT), Zech. 3:2 (NLT), Jude 1:4 (NLT), Luke 22:53, Isa. 14:9 (NLT), (Wise, 2006, Chapter 1 & 2), Ezek. 26:20 (NLT), Ps. 115:17 (NLT)

public view. Anything and everything that speaks and makes reference to God will be removed from sight.[88]

You shall take your stand against God and the Anointed One; you shall blaspheme the Holy Spirit, and you will fight against the Lords anointed followers, and what does the scripture say? "Why do the nations rage and the peoples plot in vain?" You were all born with sin; the scripture says all have sinned. You are all marked with eternal sin. You are fools, you are stupid and you reject the knowledge of the truth that "everyone who speaks a word against the Son of Man will be forgiven, but anyone who blasphemes against the Holy Spirit will not be forgiven". You perish because of your lack of knowledge. You belong to be where the un-repented fools go. You all have the spirit of Korah, you belong in the pit. You shall gain your knowledge in hell. In the fire you will have understanding, you are doomed.[89]

88 Rev. 20:13 (NLT), Num. 16:32 (NLT), Prob. 1:12 (NLT), Prov. 27:20 (ESV), 1 John 2:16 (NIV), Prov. 30:15-16 (NIV), Hab. 2:5 (NIV), Ps. 10:4 (NLT), Ps. 14:1 (NIV), Ps. 10:13 (NIV),

89 Ps. 2:1 (NIV), Rom. 3:23 (NIV), Mark 3:29 (ESV), Luke 12:10 (NIV), Prov. 10:21 (NASB), Num. 16:27, 32-33 (NIV), Job 3:26 (NIV)

Bob Jackson

The Thoughts of Your Enemy - The Ruler of foul Spirits

Review the scriptures and references listed for each paragraph in the footnotes for essay 21. Study them, think on them, speak them out loud, and meditate on them.

What are foul spirits?

"When Jesus saw that a crowd was rapidly gathering, He rebuked the unclean spirit, saying to it, "You deaf and mute spirit, I command you, come out of him and do not enter him again". Mark 9:25.

What will be their end?

"And he cried mightily with a strong voice, saying, Babylon the great is fallen, is fallen, and is become the habitation of devils, and the hold of every foul spirit, and a cage of every unclean and hateful bird". Revelation 18:2.

The enemy is already defeated. His days of sin, death and destruction are coming to an end.

Essay 22: Chaos

The whole world is chaotic, all of creation is moaning for the revealing of the sons of God. You are in the pains of childbirth. There are miseries set before you. Does not the scripture say "For nation will rise in arms against nation, and kingdom against kingdom? There will be earthquakes in various places; there will be famines. These miseries are but like the early pains of childbirth". You shall suffer, you who are called the children of God, you whom the Father loves. You know the Father and He loves you. I will use those who do not know the Father and they will steal from you, they shall kill you, and they will destroy all that the Father gives you. I want control of your mind, I want control of your body, and you shall have no hope.[90]

I have an offensive attack against all the nations on earth; I will control all the unbelieving rulers and force them to inspire the people who do not love the Lord to take a stand against His anointed. I will set the nations to devise a plan of destruction and the unbelieving populations will plot against you because they hate God just like I do. They are my followers and they do what I tell them to do, I am their father and they will carry out my desires. I will bring stress to the nations. I will entice them to fulfill my immoral desires. I will cause bewilderment in God's creation; I will initiate perplexity, puzzlement and mystification. I will create uncertainty, misunderstanding and chaos. I will be exalted above all creation; I will be like the Most High God. You will worship me or die.[91]

---

90   Rom. 8:19 & 22 (ESV), Matt. 24:8 (WEY), Mark 13:8 (WEY), 1 John 3:1 (NIV), 1 Pet. 1:13 (NIV)
91   Ps. 2:2 (NIV), Ps. 2:1 (NIV), Ps. 46:6 (NIV), John 8:44 (NIV), James 1:15 (ISV), Isa. 59:4 (NIV), (Shoebat & Richardson, 2010, Chapter 35)

I will show you some things, things that are in my power to give you. I can give you the world, with all of its beauty and riches, but you must bow down and worship me. The earth is mine, the world is mine, the Lord gave it to man and I took it from him, I have control of all that is on the earth and I can give it to you if you will give devotion to me. The whole world is under my influence, even the children of God have failed to regain control. The earth is mine and I will not give it back. The offspring of God have lost the earth to me; they do not know how to take it from me. They have not used their gifts so I took the earth and all that is in it and have not allowed them to get it back. I have the rules of worship.[92]

Many have already turned to me, many already worship me. Come to me I am he; I am the one whom you should worship. In your short life on earth, turn to me, worship me and I will give you many things and you will live a happy life before you die and receive your just reward. You shall be with me and a third of the stars who fell with me. Your reward is the bottomless pit. I cannot defeat God, but I can defeat you and make you suffer for all eternity, I do this to you because I Hate Love. God is love and God loves you. I hate God, I hate Jesus, I hate the Holy Spirit and I hate you and all that you love. [93]

92 Matt. 8:9-10 (NIV), Ps. 24:1 (NIV), Luke 19:10 (NIV), Matt. 28:18-20, John 17:18 (NIV), Isa. 29:13 (ESV), Mark 7:7 (ESV)
93 1 Tim. 5:15 (NASB), Gal. 6:7 (ERV), Matt, 4:1 (NASB), 1 John 4:16 (NIV), Rev. 9:2 (NASB), Rev. 12:9 (NIV)

The Thoughts on Essay 22

THE ENEMY – CREATING CHAOS – WHAT DO YOU THINK?

The world is in chaos because it does not know the truth and it does not have peace, there is no safety, and there is no security, nothing but danger all around us. All the Nations are in trouble. Consider the following scriptures:

"The nations are in chaos, and their kingdoms crumble! God's voice thunders and the earth melt!" Psalm 46:6.

"The kings of the earth take their stand and the rulers gather together against the LORD and against his Anointed One". Psalm 2:2.

"The city writhes in chaos; every home is locked to keep out intruders". Isaiah 24:10.

"The fortress will be abandoned, the noisy city deserted; citadel and watchtower will become a wasteland forever, the delight of donkeys, a pasture for flocks," Isaiah 24:14.

The enemy is jealous, why?

"The highest heavens belong to the LORD, but the earth he has given to man". Psalm 115:16.

The enemy does not own anything, he has nothing because of his rebellion, and therefore all he can do is create chaos and steal, kill and destroy.

What are you thinking?

Review the scriptures of the footnotes for essay 22, review the references as well.

Essay 23: Intense Hostility

I was the anointed cherub who covers; the Lord had placed me in that position. I was on the holy mountain of God; I walked in the midst of the stones of fire. God expelled me in disgrace from the mount of God. Me a guardian cherub, dismissed from among the fiery stones. I was in Eden, the garden of God; every precious stone adorned me: ruby, topaz and emerald, chrysolite, onyx and jasper, sapphire, turquoise and beryl. My settings and mountings were made of gold; on the day I was created they were prepared. I was beautiful, I was anointed. And now I have fallen from heaven; yes it is I, Lucifer, son of the morning. I was cut down to the ground, and I have weakened the nations. And Jesus saw me; He was watching me fall from heaven like lightning.[94]

So, here I am, no more Lucifer the beautiful cherub. I am now to be known as the great dragon that was thrown down, the serpent of old who is called the devil and Satan, who deceives the whole world; I was thrown down to the earth, and my angels were thrown down with me. I spoke to the created women in the Garden of Eden and through her I was able to get to the man that God had created, their rebellion allowed me to get control of the earth. I tried a different but similar tactic with the Lord Jesus and was rebuked. I could not get Him to sin, He defeated me with scripture. I was ordered to leave Him and I did. I am now the god of this world and I have blinded the minds of the unbelievers, to keep them from seeing the light of the gospel of the glory of Christ, who is the image of God.[95]

---

94 Ezek. 28:14 (NASB), Ezek. 28:16 (NIV), Ezek. 28:13 (NIV), Isa. 14:12 (KJB), Luke 10:18 (NIV),
95 Rev.12:9 (NASB), Gen. 3:1 (NIV), Matt. 4:10 (NIV)

I want their eyes closed; I want their eyes open only to darkness. I want them under my power, the power of Satan and not God; I do not want them to receive forgiveness of sins and a place among those who are sanctified by faith in Jesus. I have many schemes, and I can outwit Gods creation, I have all unbelievers blinded. The only light you unbelievers will ever see is the light shining bright in your eternal home. You shall see the light of hell in the midst of darkness, you shall smell the stench of hell, you shall hear the screams of hell, and you shall thirst and be tormented forever. You shall be with me in the lake of fire and brimstone. No one can save you, there is no relief, no rest, nothing but misery forever.[96]

---

96 Acts 26:18 (NIV), 2 Cor. 4:4 (NIV)

Bob Jackson

The Thoughts on Essay 23

THE ENEMY'S INTENSE HOSTILITY TOWARDS GOD AND MAN

What is this intense love God has for Man? We know that God is love.

"So we have come to know and to believe the love that God has for us. God is love, and whoever abides in love abides in God, and God abides in him". 1 John 4:16.

"Don't you see how wonderfully kind, tolerant, and patient God is with you? Does this mean nothing to you? Can't you see that his kindness is intended to turn you from your sin?" Romans 2:4.

What is this intense aggression the enemy has toward God and Man? We know that Satan is the opposite of love.

"And the great dragon was cast down, the old serpent, he that is called the Devil and Satan, the deceiver of the whole world; he was cast down to the earth, and his angels were cast down with him". Revelation 12:9.

We are in a war with a stubborn defeated foe that will fight until his end comes. "Everyone who competes in the games goes into strict training. They do it to get a crown that will not last; but we do it to get a crown that will last forever". 1 Corinthians 9:25.

Resist the enemy and take no prisoners.

Review the scripture's in the footnotes

74

Essay 24: I Hate You

Before you were formed in your mother's womb, before you were born I conspired to steal, kill and destroy you, I planned to keep you from knowing and being used by God to increase His kingdom. I plotted to have you stolen, I schemed to have you diseased, and I strategized to have you deformed and miserable. I wanted more than anything else to take your life by any means necessary; I designed plans to take away your parents, your guardians, any and all who would lead you to wisdom, understanding and peace. I wanted to keep you from salvation. I wanted to see you grow-up in this world without hope, why should God be pleased with you? I wanted to see you grow without the knowledge of God through Jesus.[97]

God has seen your unformed body; and in His book He has written your days, long before they actually occur. Yes, the Lord has shaped you; He has made you. But, I am always plotting to destroy you. Your days are numbered and I want to use you and then get rid of you. I do not want you to even try to understand the workings of God. My world does not want another prophet of God. I hate you, the whole world hates you. I do not want you to be appointed over my nations and kingdoms, I do not want them displaced and torn down, they must not be destroyed and overthrown, and I do not want you to build and to plant the things of God. This is my kingdom. Your name will not be made known in my domain; your name shall not be mentioned. You will not be called; I have blinded

---

97 Jer. 1:5 (NIV), Ps. 127:3-5 (NIV), Lev. 18:21 (NIV), 2 Kings 15:16 (NIV) Amos 1:13 (ESV), Prov. 22:6 (ESV), Eph. 6:4 (ESV), 1 Cor. 8:3 (NIV), Gal. 1:15 (NIV)

you to the truth. You will die ignorant. I have captured your mind and made you my slave.[98]

This is my struggle against the Lord. This is my struggle against the Lords anointed. My goal is to bring terror upon you, I will harass you, and I will cause sickness and plagues to come upon you. I have control of all the powers that be both religious and secular. I know everything about you; I know everything that you do, everyplace that you go. I know what you eat and where you sleep, what you wear, what you say. I know all your dirty little secrets. I am not like the Most High God who knows your heart, but I am the god of this world and I have established a worldwide system that will provide me information to access and control your life. I can see all and know all just like Father God. I am "Big Brother" and I am watching you always. God loves you with an everlasting love, but I hate you with an everlasting hatred. You will hate the God of love and by your rejection, you will worship me.[99]

I have introduced major problems among you. Abortions, kidnappings, loneliness, desertions, disease, hunger, abused, murder, stealing, greed, envy and other abominable things such as war, rape, false teaching. Because of your sin, you have given yourself and this world to me. You have rejected your creator and have come to me. I do not love you, I hate you and I will show no mercy while you live and after you die.[100]

---

98 Ps. 139:16 (NASB), Job 10:8 (NIV), Job 14:5 (NIV), Eccles. 11:5 (NIV), Ps. 119:73 (NIV), Jer. 1:10 (NIV), Isa. 49:1 (NIV)

99 Job 11:20 (NIV), (Gabriel, 2006, Chapter 9), (Jeffrey, 2009, Chapter 4), Jer. 31:3 (ESV)

100 2 Thess. 1:8 (NIV), Lam. 5:12 (NIV), Isa. 9:17 (ESV), Isa. 1:4 (NIV), Prov. 21:13 (NIV), Eccles. 9:12 (NIV),

The Thoughts on Essay 24

The enemy's thoughts concerning how much he hates you should give you pause to think, Selah.

1.   The enemy hates you for the following reasons:

"You love righteousness and hate wickedness; therefore God, your God, has set you above your companions by anointing you with the oil of joy". Psalm 45:7.

"At one time we too were foolish, disobedient, deceived and enslaved by all kinds of passions and pleasures. We lived in malice and envy, being hated and hating one another". Titus 3:3.

"You used to walk in these ways, in the life you once lived". Colossians 3:7.

2.   The enemy remembers when you were of the world. You belonged to a special group among his followers:

"They are the kind who worm their way into homes and gain control over weak-willed women, who are loaded down with sins and are swayed by all kinds of evil desires,". 2 Timothy 3:6.

"They claim to know God, but by their actions they deny him. They are detestable, disobedient and unfit for doing anything good". Titus 1:16.

3.   And what do these scriptures teach us?

"It teaches us to say "No" to ungodliness and worldly passions, and to live self-controlled, upright and godly lives in this present age," Titus 2:12.

This is why you are hated by the enemy. You are being taught by the Spirit to have the mind of Christ. The enemy would rather see you dead in your sins and condemned to an everlasting hell.

Think about it?

Essay 25: My Kingdom Come

I desire to build my kingdom and keep it. I will form my kingdom by waging war against the Lords creation and against His anointed ones. I know that all humans will give up everything to save their own life. I will force them to join my kingdom. I will inflict damage to their bodies, they shall be covered with worms and scabs, their skin will be broken and decayed. They will waste away, they will burn with fever. I shall afflict them from the soles of their feet to the top of their head, there will be no completeness only wounds and welts and open sores. They shall cry out in pain, they shall have no rest. I shall destroy the physical beauty of God's creation.[101]

I shall take control of you. I will go through you as wheat. I will make you do things against those you love. You shall become like me, a liar and a deceiver. You will be under my power, blinded, kept in darkness, you shall not see the light, and you will not be seated among those who are sanctified by faith in Jesus. Come to me, I will help you develop your sinful nature; I will show you how to handle your self- control. I am much smarter than you; you are no match for me, I have many ideas for your life, ideas that will suit my purposes. I am the angel of light, I will lead you. I have a message for you. You will be shocked when you feel it. It is eternal fire, it is prepared for me and my angels, but I will be more than happy to share it with you. I lost my place in heaven. If I cannot be there, neither will you. The earth is mind, the air is mind and you shall do my bidding.[102]

---

101 (Shoebat & Richardson, 2010, Chapter 64), Job 2:4-5 (NASB), Job 2:7 (NASB), Job 7: 5 (NASB), Job 13:28 (NASB), Job 7:13 (NASB), Job 30:30 (NASB), Isa 1:6 (NASB), 1 Sam. 14:25 (NASB)

102 Luke 22:3 (NIV), Luke 22:31 (NIV), John 13:27 (NIV), Acts 5:3 (NIV), Acts 26:18 (NIV), 1 Cor. 7:5 (NIV), 2 Cor. 2:11 (NIV), 2 Cor. 11:14 (NIV), 2 Cor. 12:7 (NIV), Matt. 25:41 (NIV), Rev. 12:8 (NIV), Rev. 12:12 (NIV)

I am the great dragon. I was thrown down—I am that ancient serpent called the devil, or Satan, who leads the whole world astray. I was tossed to the earth, and my angels with me. This is my kingdom. I am the prince of this world; I will resist being removed as long as possible, I will not be driven out. Your minds must be led astray from sincere and pure devotion to Christ. It was the Lord Jesus who saw me fall from heaven like lightening to the earth. I am full of fury and rage. I am too proud to give up or admit defeat. This battle between me and the Lord must continue and you will help me to keep it going. I will wage war against the Lords anointed. It is you He is using to defeat me; therefore I must wage war on His holy ones. The Gospel must be stopped. I have control of the unbelievers, I have control of the unsaved, I have control of all those who live by reason and rationalization, those who reject the foolishness of the Gospel and have not place their trust in the Lord Jesus Christ. These are my followers, these are my disciples.[103]

I must continuously attack the Christian soldier, I must weaken their battle plan, and I must tear down the solid foundation which is built on the Word of God. I will continue my strategy to resist the truth and spread error through every type of evil communication my forces can create. We shall force them to endure hardship; we shall see if they can tolerate suffering, we shall see if they can remain faithful to the Gospel of Christ. We will see if they can stand against my flaming arrows.[104]

---

103 Rev. 12:9 (NIV), John 12:31 (NIV), 2 Cor. 11:3 (NIV), Luke 10:18 (NIV),
104 (Phillips, 2010, Chapter 28), 2 Tim. 2:3-4 (NIV), Eph. 6:16 (NIV),

The Thoughts on Essay 25

Think about your adversary's fall-What can be learned from it?

Consider this. A superior angel was created in the midst of all the other angels. He was the most beautiful angel ever fashioned by God. He was framed in precious stones, perfect jewels of many varieties, he was fitted in gold that was flawless, he was beautiful, and he was a unique cherub. He walked in the middle of the stones of fire. He was anointed to cover his assigned regions; he was in Eden the garden of God. He was in Gods Holy Mountain, he was blameless in his ways, he was the minster of worship and he had the seal of excellence. Ezekiel 28:11-19.

What happen?

He exercised his free will to rebel against his Creator. He was full of pride and the scripture in Ezekiel 28:15 says that unrighteousness was found in him. In examining the synonyms related to unrighteousness we can see that there were some very serious character flaws. He had a dark side, there was blackness. He had become evil, immoral, iniquitous, nefarious, and rotten.

This once exquisite cherub had become sinful, unethical, unlawful, bad and unsavory. What this unbelieving world is now being faced with is a vicious, vile, villainous, wicked and wrong spirited fiend.

He tried to seize the thrown of God. He persuaded one third of the angels of heaven and attempted a mutiny against his Maker. "What arrogance".

This is our enemy. We are to resist, adapt and overcome. Read and study Ephesians 6:11-18.

Please remember this, "We fight from Jesus Christ victory over the enemy". (Phillips, 2010, Chapter 30)

Essay 26: This is your Eternal Home

"Many live their entire lives wanting nothing to do with God. They don't acknowledge that Jesus is God, and they never pray or read the Bible". Many of you will enter hell by default. I look at Gods creation and can see that because they never make a decision to believe and trust in Jesus, they virtually seal their own fate. They ignore the fact that Jesus is Father Gods appointed way to Himself. They make no decision. And by making no decision they decide to spend eternity with me and my demons in the lake of fire. God does not send them to hell; they choose to go to hell and all the time blaming and cursing God because they made a bad choice.[105]

Men are foolish, they are quick to believe a lie, and they are quick to reject the truth. They spend their lives worshiping created things, objects, people, and animals. They worship idols, things of wood covered with metal, statures, graven images, singers, musicians, actors, politicians, sports, wise men, people of knowledge and wealth. You believe your religion or intellect will save you. This is your lot, this is the portion the LORD has decreed for you, and this is done because you have forgotten Him and trusted in false gods. We are waiting for you. There are demons ready to deal with you; they have been given permission to torment you until the time comes when we all will be tormented together. A place where the worm does not die and the fire is not quenched; there is no hope, no mercy, no peace, no purpose and no rest. Nothing but foul spirits live in your new home, nothing but stench and vulgar, blasphemous language, all sorts of profanity. You lived your life on earth this way and you will die and sing the choruses of torment and misery.[106]

---

105 (Wise, 2008, Chapter 9), John 3:18 (NASB), Matt. 7:13-14 (NASB), Rom. 1:25 (NIV)

106 Rom. 1:25 (NIV), Jer. 13:25 (NIV), Matt. 25:41 (NIV), (Wise, 2006, Chapter 10), Mark 9:44 (NASB), Mark 9:25 (NIV), Rev. 18:2 (NIV)

In that day, when the LORD shuts the gates of hell, I will be your choir director for all eternity, we the condemned being constantly plagued and distressed will sing the songs of agony and pain, we shall follow the melody of profanity and shout about our sorrows of doom and gloom in an environment of fire and brimstone filled with stink and horrible punishment, forever and ever shall we sing the deafening chants of the lost. All my demons who; cannot not find rest in this waterless place will find it by controlling your souls. Your eternal state will be worse than you can ever imagine, you shall sing the hymns of the dammed for all eternity. All hope is gone; the God you ignored in life is now honoring your choice to be left alone. [107]

107 2 Thess.1:8 (NIV), Mark 9:48 (NIV), Jude 1:7 (NIV), Isa. 13:8 (NIV), Luke 11:24, (Phillips, 2010, pg.4)

What Are Your Thoughts About Man's Present Condition and His Future Eternal Home?

Heaven or Hell which one will you choose?

You must understand that you will live forever. You must realize that you need to choose the one who lives forever and ever. "I am the Living One; I was dead, and behold I am alive for ever and ever! And I hold the keys of death and Hades". Revelation 1:18.

You are already condemned. But the Father has provided a way for you to escape the guilty verdict. "Whoever believes in the Son has eternal life, but whoever rejects the Son will not see life, for God's wrath remains on him". 1 John 5:12.

You have three choices to choose from, Jesus, Satan or neither.

1. If you choose Jesus. You get a free gift, you do not earn it and you do not deserve it. "For the wages of sin is death, but the free gift of God is eternal life in Christ Jesus our Lord". Romans 6:23.

2. If you choose Satan. This is your warning, "You belong to your father, the devil, and you want to carry out your father's desire. He was a murderer from the beginning, not holding to the truth, for there is no truth in him. When he lies, he speaks his native language, for he is a liar and the father of lies". John 8:44.

3. If you are an atheist, religious or you decide to make no choice. You need to consider the following: You are a fool. "The fool has said in his heart, "There is no God." They are corrupt, and have done abominable iniquity. There is no one who does good". Psalm 53:1. Do not expect your religion, good deeds or good behavior to become a mediator between you and God. "For there is only one God and one Mediator who can reconcile God and humanity--the man Christ Jesus". 1 Timothy 2:5. Making no choice means that you have refused Gods free gift of eternal live and you defaulted yourself to Satan.

Please choose life!

Conclusion

I end these essays with this final warning to all those who are "active" spirit filled soldiers of Christ. I quote from Pastor Ron Phillips. "Just because a person waves a Bible and act spiritually does not mean that their ministry is anointed by God. Religious deception is the worst of all demonic control". (Phillips, 2010, Chapter 13)

We must remember that Deception is the enemy's tool; it is his weapon of choice. The scripture warns us about being taken advantage of. It says, "Do not let him gain the advantage over you; do not be ignorant of his devices". 2 Cor. 2:11.

We must remember to avoid quarreling among ourselves. The scripture warns us that, "No doubt there have to be differences among you to show which of you have God's approval". 1 Corinthians 11:19.

We are at war with the devil and his demons. We are soldiers of Christ. We are His Ambassadors. Fight the enemy with the Word of God. Resist, Make the devil flee from you. James 4:7. Adapt spiritual words to spiritual truths. 1 Corinthians 2:13. And overcome evil with good. Romans 12:21.

We must remember that we are an offensive army not a defensive one (Phillips, 2010, Chapter 32). We are attacking the kingdom of darkness; we are well armed with the Word of God, operating under the power of the Holy Spirit laying siege to the enemy's wicked empire, tearing down its strongholds (2 Cor. 10:4), busting through its gates (Matt.16:18) to rescue the perishing. Let us not forget what hymnist (Fanny J. Crosby) texted in her hymn,

Rescue the perishing, care for the dying,
Snatch them in pity from sin and the grave;
Weep o'er the erring one, lift up the fallen,
Tell them of Jesus, the mighty to save.
Rescue the perishing, care for the dying;
Jesus is merciful, Jesus will save.

Jude 23 tells us to snatch others from the fire and save them.

When Jesus returns to establish His earthly kingdom, the kingdom of darkness will be sacked. Until then, complete your mission, discover your spiritual gifts and work in that ministry. Occupy (Luke 19:13) and do all in the name of Jesus, amen.

Personal Testimony

I was raised up as a Roman Catholic and attended a Catholic School because my mother and father wanted their children to receive a good education. There are four of us, myself, two sisters and a brother. I received a good education; I learned a lot about the catholic religion, I knew I was a sinner, I learned a little about Jesus, a little about Father God, a little about the Holy Ghost and a lot about Mary and the Saints of the Catholic Church. I was taught religion and tradition.

I wanted to know God; I was looking for Him during my early years of life. I had religion, but I did not have God. I was searching for Him. I was growing up in the world and going in the wrong direction learning the philosophies of men and following their practices.

After graduating high school I enlisted in the US Navy and completed two tours to Viet Nam obeying and following convention. I was still searching for God and "not realizing it" following the devil at the same time. After I was honorably discharged from military service, I decided to go to College and study mechanical technology and then continued on to study mechanical engineering. I graduated and worked in industry and for the US Government.

During my time as an engineer in industry, I was introduced to the gospel of the Lord Jesus Christ by my boss's secretary. I attended the bible studies they had during lunch hour and before long I accepted Christ as my Lord and savior. "Finally", I found Father God through accepting His Son the Lord Jesus. John 3:16 opened my eyes and led my heart to the path of salvation.

I continued on with my education and received my master's degree in Telecommunications and made an attempt to work on a PhD until I finally realized I had enough of this worldly education. I was tired of the philosophies of this world and the traditions of the educational system and the outrageous cost which leads to bondage. It is time to do what the Lord wants me to do. Plant the seed of the gospel and open the eyes of the lost so that they can see the truth and live forever with the one who loves us with an everlasting Love.

I ask you two (??) questions.

1. Have you come to that place in your spiritual life where you know for certain that if you were to die tonight you would go to heaven?

2. And if you were to die tonight, what would you say to God as to why He should let you into His Heaven?

If you cannot answer these questions, May I suggest to you that you better know for certain where you are going to spend eternity?

Consider these scriptures. John 3:36 and John 3:16, read them, study them, meditate on them. Now take action and make your decision. Begin your spiritual journey by reading the entire Bible starting from Genesis to Revelation, plan on accomplishing the reading in one year.

God bless you
Bob Jackson, Ambassador for Christ,
E-mail: roberay60@gmail.com

References

The Holy Bible

List of Abbreviations & Versions

1. NIV New International Version

2. ESV English Standard Version

3. NAS New American Standard Bible

4. NLT New Living Translation

5. GWT God's Word Translation

6. KJV King James Version

7. ASV American Standard Version

8. ISV International Standard Version

9. BIBE Bible In Basic English

10. KJB King James Bible

11. NASB New American Standard Bible

12. AMP Amplified Bible

13. AKJV American King James Version

14. DRB Douay-Rheims Bible

15. DBY Darby Bible Translation

16. ERV English Revised Version

17. WEB

Annotated Bibliography

1. Anderson, N. T. (2000). Victory over Darkness: Realizing the power of your identity in Christ. Regal Books: Ventura, CAL.

Discovering who you are in Christ and gaining success over darkness

2. Bevere, J. (2001). Under Cover: The Promise of Protection under His Authority. Thomas Nelson, Inc.: Nashville, TEN.

The clandestine tactics of the enemy against believers

3. Bonnke, R. (1996). Evangelism by Fire: Inviting Your Passion for the Lost. Reinhard Bonnke Ministries: Sacramento, CA.

The will to evangelize to lost souls in power and with faith

4. Enlow, J. (2008).The Seven Mountain Prophecy: Unveiling the Coming Elijah Revolution. Creation House: Lake Mary, FLA.

In this book the author attempts to bring the reader face-to-face with the coming Tishbite transformation. An event now in effect that encourages the Saints to strike with force the seven mountains of worldly influence that has a destructive effect on our everyday life.

5. Gabriel, B. (2006). Because They Hate: A Survivor of Islamic Terror Warns America. St. Martin's Press: New York, N.Y.

This book is an eye-witness testimony concerning Islamic hatred.

6. Jeffrey, G. R. (2009). Shadow Government: How the Secret Global Elite is Using Surveillance against You. Water brook Press: Colorado Springs, CO.

The author presents facts concerning worldwide surveillance of the population's habits.

7. Meyer, J. (1995). Battlefield of the mind: Winning the Battle in Your Mind. Faith Words Hachette Book Group: NY, NY.

Identifying and conquering wrong thought patterns. Gives a good explanation as to why we should control our thoughts.

8. Phillips, R. (2010). Demons: Spiritual Warfare. Charisma House: Lake Mary, FLA.

The author provides modest, influential implements for beating Satan in our everyday living.

9. Sears, A., Osten, C. (2003). The Homosexual Agenda: Exposing the Principal Threat to Religious Freedom Today. B & H Publishing Group: Nashville, TEN.

This book discusses the homosexual agenda and its attempt to defeat those in opposition to it.

10. Sutherland, M. I. (2005). Judicial Tyranny: the new kings of America? Amerisearch, Inc. St. Louis, MO.

These writings discuss the judicial systems attack on morality. The authors confer how the judiciary is establishing itself as the tyrannical authority of America

11. Taylor, K. (2004). Brainwashing: The science of thought control. Oxford University Press: New York, NY.

Discovering things that materialize when the human mind is changed by external powers

12. Shoebat, W., Richardson, J. (2010). God's War on Terror: Islam, Prophecy and the Bible. Top Executive Media.

The authors talk about End-Time Prophecy concerning the Nation of Islam

13. Wiese, B. (2008). Hell. Charisma House: Lake Mary, FLA.

The author gives his personal testimony about things he saw in a place that many believe does not exist. Many will end up in that place by choice and by default.

14. Wise, B. (2006). 23 Minutes in Hell. Charisma House: Lake Mary, FLA.

The author's story of what he saw, heard, and felt in the place of torment.

Electronic Reference

1. Association of Zoos & Aquariums (n.d.). African Wild Dogs - Species Survival Guide. Retrieved from http://www.aza.org/cef-awarded-project-summaries/.

2. Biblos.com (2004-2011). Search, Read, Study the Bible in Many Languages. http://biblos.com/.

3. Merriam-Webster (2011). Dictionary. Retrieved April 9, 2011. http://www.merriam-webster.com/dictionary/.

4. Moloch. Encyclopedia Mythical. Retrieved March 02, 2011, from Encyclopedia Mythical Online. http://www.pantheon.org/articles/m/moloch.html.

5. Ask.com (2011). Ask your question? Retrieved April 18, 2011. http://www.ask.com/web?qsrc=2105&o=0&l=dir&dm=&q=tyrant%20definition.

6. National Geographic (1996-2001). Wild Dogs. Retrieved April 22, 2011, http://animals.nationalgeographic.com/animals/photos/wild-dogs/#/african-wild-dogs_441_600x450.jpg.

7. Vines Expository Dictionary: Old and New Testament words. http://www2.mf.no/bibel/vines.html.

8. Photos of Biblical Explanations Pt.1: Lake of Fire: Windows Internet Explorer. Retrieved July 23, 2011, http://photosofbiblicalexplanations1.blogspot.com/2011/04/lake-of-fire.html.

9. Bible Encyclopedia. http://www.christiananswers.net/dictionary/leviathan.html.

10. Fanny J. Crosby (1820-1915). Rescue the Perishing. Retrieved September 23, 2011, http://www.hymnsite.com/lyrics/umh591.sht.